This is dedicated to all the students who will love, hate, dream, laugh, and cry their way through their middle school years. Just like we all have.

And to the staff at Meriwether Publishing, Ltd. for believing I had another 102 monologues left in me.

And lastly to my family and friends for encouraging me. I love you all.

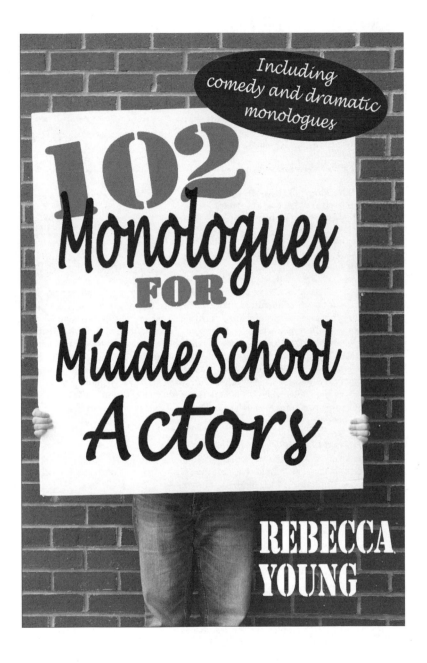

Including comedy and dramatic monologues

102 Monologues FOR Middle School Actors

REBECCA YOUNG

MERIWETHER PUBLISHING LTD.
Colorado Springs, Colorado

Meriwether Publishing Ltd., Publisher
PO Box 7710
Colorado Springs, CO 80933-7710

www.meriwether.com

Editor: Theodore O. Zapel
Assistant editor: Amy Hammelev
Cover design: Jan Melvin

Library of Congress Cataloging-in-Publication Data

Young, Rebecca, 1965-
  102 monologues for middle school actors : including comedy and dramatic monologues / by Rebecca Young. -- 1st ed.
      p. cm.
  ISBN 978-1-56608-184-9
  1. Monologues. 2. Dialogues. 3. Acting. I. Title. II. Title: One hundred and two monologues for middle school actors. III. Title: One hundred two monologues for middle school actors.
  PN2080.Y665 2012
  812'.6--dc23

                                                    2012001050

1   2   3   12   13   14

CONTENTS

Introduction

There's nothing more frustrating than trying to perform a monologue that doesn't speak your language. That's why *102 Monologues for Middle School Actors* is an important resource for young students. Written in the voice of teenage characters, it emphasizes believable teenage experiences that appeal to young actors. All monologues are age appropriate and range from comedic to dramatic.

It's been a long, long while since the days I walked the hallways of a middle school. Why then are those memories still vivid in my mind? Probably because those days spent moving on from elementary school and gearing up for high school are some of the best and hardest times a student can go through.

102 Monologues for Middle School Actors brings those bittersweet memories to life. Boyfriend issues, girlfriend issues. Teacher issues, parent issues. Sports issues, band issues. Love, hate, jealousy, betrayal, and so much more. With 102 realistic scenes to choose from, one is guaranteed to speak to you!

1. Allergic to Anesthesia

(Girl or Guy)

1 So you know how most people break out in a rash or
2 their throat closes up and they can't swallow when they
3 have an allergic reaction to something? Well, I wish that was
4 me. I'm being completely serious! That's how normal people
5 should react.

6 Take an antihistamine or at worst get a shot from an
7 EpiPen and bam! Back to normal. Not me. I could never
8 have a normal reaction to anything. Who would believe that
9 a person could be allergic to anesthesia anyway? And who
10 else would go crazy from it? No one else. That's who.

11 And I'm talking all kinds of crazy. One minute I'm
12 laughing, the next minute I'm crying. Then after that I'm
13 super jacked up paranoid. Like for real I thought my mom
14 was trying to steal my shoelaces. I got all hysterical over
15 stupid grotty shoelaces that even a homeless person
16 wouldn't want!

17 And when my friends came by to visit me, guess what I
18 did? I sang to them! Me. The one who can't sing in the
19 shower because I'd want to drown myself. And then,
20 because that's just not bad enough, I had to burst into
21 tears because they brought me a balloon in the shape of a
22 turtle. Now who in the world cries over a sweet jolly-faced
23 turtle?!

24 Want to know the absolute worst part? I have to have
25 surgery again — and all my friends and half the school can't
26 wait to come see me. I may just have to hang a "Do Not
27 Disturb" sign on my door or I may have to quit school!

2. De-Friend Me! Well, I'll De-Friend You!

(Girl or Guy)

1   On Saturday I had four hundred and fifty-two friends.
2 Not all of them bona fide, I-know-them-by-heart friends, but
3 friends of friends and friends of friends' friends. I was feeling
4 pretty good about my social media popularity. I had more
5 than most of my friends and some of them were even
6 desperate enough to add people that nobody even knew.
7 Pathetic.
8   That was Saturday.
9   Today I am down to one hundred and twelve friends.
10 That's right, I've lost over three hundred friends! All
11 because of a stupid fight I had with a handful of people. It
12 started what I call the "De-friend Disaster of _____" *(Insert*
13 *current year).*
14   See all I did was de-friend Scott, Allison, Mark, and
15 Caroline. And I had a right to! They picked each other for
16 the class project and left me to be with the loser group. You
17 know the ones. Slackers. Underachievers. The kind of group
18 that will make *me* do all the work.
19   "We could only have four," my so-called friends told me.
20 Well, why wasn't I the fourth? Or the third? Why couldn't
21 they have left Allison out of the group? So I de-friended
22 them. Clearly they aren't really my friends anyway.
23   Well when their friends saw that I wasn't friends with
24 them anymore, they de-friended me. And then when the
25 friends of their friends saw it, they de-friended me. On and
26 on until over three hundred people deleted me from their
27 friends list.

1   Do you know how pathetic it is to have only one hundred
2   plus friends? My grandma has more than that. And half her
3   friends are dead!
4   I think I'm going to have to delete my page altogether. I
5   can't have kids at school seeing my low friend count. They'll
6   think I'm a loser. No one — not even my little sister who
7   isn't even supposed to have a page — has so few friends. At
8   least if I'm not on there, no one else can de-friend me.

3. Bed Bugs

(Guy)

1   Look at me. What do you see? A kid that looks like
2 someone had a field day with a red marker, right? At best I
3 look like a bad case of chicken pox. Or maybe someone who
4 spent the night inside a glass cage filled with mosquitoes.
5 I'm covered in spots. I have literally counted over five
6 hundred spots — and that's just on my legs! In fact you can
7 barely see normal skin underneath all these red spots.

8   And man do they itch. Until you scratch them too much
9 and then they hurt like heck! So you want to know how I got
10 this way? It wasn't the chicken pox like my grandma said.
11 And it wasn't mosquitoes. Or chiggers. Or any other normal
12 kind of bugs.

13   Oh no. My dad has to go on lots of business trips and
14 he was kind enough to bring home a gift that keeps on
15 giving — *bed bugs!* Thanks a lot Dad. Our whole house has
16 them now and we can't get rid of them. And when I asked
17 my grandma if I could stay at her house, she said no. She
18 doesn't want to risk getting them. Now I don't really blame
19 her. But *come on!* What grandma says no to her one and
20 only grandson?!

21   All I know is, if my parents don't find a way to get rid of
22 these critters soon, I'm setting the house on fire! I mean it
23 ... *(Turn to left as if you just saw someone.)*
24   No! Wait! Mr. Turner! I was just kidding. No need to call
25 the police. I promise. I am not going to set my house on fire!
26 *(Rush Off-Stage yelling)*

4. Maybe I'll Be a Leftie

(Girl or Guy)

1   I remember when I was little I would always try to write
2 with my left hand. I'd practice writing my name over and
3 over to see if I could get it to look anything like when I did
4 it right-handed. It never did. Now I'm wishing that I had tried
5 even harder. But who knew it would matter so much?

6   I'm about to give up on my right wrist ever working the
7 way it should again. The doctor has had three chances
8 already to get it right. Three surgeries — on one tiny little
9 wrist! How complicated can it be? And now he wants to do
10 one more. "The final one," he says. Haven't I heard that
11 before? Wasn't the last one supposed to be the final one?
12 And the one before that? Does the dude have a new boat he
13 needs to pay for or maybe he's got some kind of trophy wife
14 that needs a lot of plastic surgery? Whatever the reason, I
15 think he's enjoying all this money my parents are giving
16 him. I'm pretty sure he's in there creating problems instead
17 of fixing them!

18   And this time I get the added benefit of getting fifty
19 percent less mobility. That sounds like a lot, doesn't it? Like
20 if you were to eat fifty percent of a pie, people would talk,
21 right? That's why I'm thinking that maybe I should just
22 become a leftie. At least my left wrist works one hundred
23 percent. It might not write as neatly, but then again who
24 knows how I'm going to write with half a wrist!

25   Let's get real. You wouldn't let someone operate so that
26 you only had fifty percent of your brain, would you? Or if
27 they could only cure fifty percent of your cancer? Or if you
28 only got to use fifty percent of your eyes! Yeah, that's right.

1   Picture walking around with a patch. Fifty percent is not a
2   fraction I'm happy about. But what choice do I have?
3   Well I tell you what. If this doesn't work, I'm getting a
4   hook!

5. The Other Daughter

(Girl)

1   Susie this and Susie that. Did you see Susie's report
2 card? Did you hear how well she did in school today? Did you
3 know she was picked to be line leader again today? Can you
4 believe it? Our little Susie?!
5   *(Roll eyes.)* Are you kidding me? You'd think my little
6 sister had just been nominated Class President of the
7 Second Grade the way my parents go on and on about her.
8 She never does anything wrong. And unfortunately that's the
9 honest to goodness truth. The little brat really never ever
10 does anything wrong. It's like she's a perfect little angel.
11 Everything she does is right. She's never been spanked,
12 grounded, or even mildly yelled at. Her whole life she's been
13 amazing. Not messing up once. Not even by accident!
14   She's never broke one of Mom's favorite dishes. She's
15 never forgotten to do her homework. She's never splashed
16 too much water on the floor during her bath. She's never
17 done anything wrong!
18   Do you have any idea what it's like being related to
19 someone like that? Do you think I don't hear the sighs my
20 mother makes? You know the one. The one that says, "Oh,
21 how I wish I had *two* perfect daughters instead of just one.
22 If only Ellie could be more like Susie." Yeah. *That* sigh.
23   It makes me want to frame the little angelic punk. Like
24 shred her homework or hide a broken dish under her bed.
25 Only I know I'd get caught. I always get caught.
26   Maybe I can talk Mom into having another kid. A normal
27 one. Only what if … oh, surely there couldn't be *two* of them!

6. Sleepovers Are for Girls!

(Guy)

1   There's a very important reason why boys should *not*
2 have sleepovers. In fact I'll go out on a limb and say
3 sleepovers should absolutely only be for girls. Want to know
4 why? Guys don't sleep. And guys are mean. And guys —
5 even your best friends in the whole school — like playing
6 pranks on you and embarrassing you in front of absolutely
7 everyone and anyone.

8   I guess it's really all my fault. I know how my friends are.
9 They're loony. Crazy. Can't be serious for half a second.
10 Stupid. I should've known they would never ever go to sleep
11 like normal people do. Especially after we drank six two-liter
12 bottles of soda, and ate three bags of chips, and two
13 packages of cookies. Between sugar and caffeine, we were
14 hyped-up pretty good. At least they were.

15   I tend to go the other way when I gorge out on food and
16 soda. I crash big time. So I'm not even sure what time I
17 actually fell asleep but I'm guessing it was sometime before
18 midnight because I remember about half of the first movie
19 we rented.

20   So my friends had way too many hours of them being
21 wide awake and me being asleep. Clearly watching the
22 movies we rented was not nearly exciting enough for them.
23 Want to know what I woke up to? A peace sign drawn on my
24 forehead with a permanent marker, one of my eyebrows
25 shaved off, my fingernails painted bright pink — thanks to
26 my sister's stash — and all of my underwear hung out in the
27 tree on the front lawn. For everyone to see. Do you know
28 how many girls live in my neighborhood? Well neither do I!

1   But I know it's more than I want to see my underwear.

2   That's why I say: New rules guys, sleepovers are for

3   girls!

7. You Call That Courtesy?

(Girl or Guy)

1   I've been robbed! Not the gun-in-your-side, give-me-
2 your-money kind of robbed, but robbed just the same. And
3 by my bank, no less. The place that is supposed to be
4 protecting my money. The place that is supposed to be
5 helping me make money. The place that is supposed to be
6 on my side!

7   I make one teensy little mistake and they charge me
8 thirty-five dollars. How do they expect me to pay that? If I
9 *had* thirty-five dollars, I wouldn't have overdrawn my
10 account! Do they know how many hours I have to babysit
11 *(Or mow lawns, if desired)* to make that kind of money? And
12 for what? To pay a fee and I don't get anything for it?

13   Well you know whose fault this really is? My dad's.
14 That's right. He's the one who said, and I quote, "You can
15 never be too young to learn financial responsibility." Well,
16 guess what Dad? You are wrong! Clearly you *can* be too
17 young to learn financial responsibility.

18   Who knew banks were so mean anyway? Don't they
19 know that people make mistakes sometimes? Couldn't
20 someone have just called me, or texted me, and told me
21 that I didn't have any money in my account? Wouldn't that
22 have been the nice thing to do? Don't they know I'll pay it
23 back as soon as I can? Don't they know that I'm just a kid?
24 How can they even call themselves a friendly small town
25 community bank? They aren't friendly at all!

26   But here's the real kicker. When I called to find out why
27 they were charging me thirty-five dollars, they said they *let*
28 me overdraw as a courtesy. How is that a courtesy? They

1   charged me thirty-five dollars to do it. That's like paying for
2   a favor! It's not a favor if you have to pay for it. I think
3   someone needs to teach these banks what courtesy really
4   means.

8. Devil Cat

(Girl)

1   My cat is evil, with a capital D. Yeah, that's right. She's
2 the *devil*. Evil incarnate. She is completely destroying my
3 room. I don't know why she's so fascinated by the posters
4 on my wall, but every night when I'm trying to sleep, she
5 jumps at the walls, claws bared, and tries to shred my
6 posters to bits. She's ruined almost every single one. And
7 that's not all. She loves unraveling the toilet paper and then
8 dragging it all over the house. Guess who gets to clean it
9 up? *Me!* I get to clean up *all* her messes — like it's my fault
10 the cat is born of the dark side.
11   Who could've known from her sweet little face and
12 unnaturally small body that she could be so devious. She
13 looks like every other cat. And she's solid white, like an
14 angel. Everyone knows that white represents good and
15 black represents evil. This cat might be total white, but her
16 soul is total black!
17   There's no way I could've known that when I got her
18 from the shelter that her sole purpose would be to destroy
19 my family's house — and my sanity!
20   She sleeps all day and then prowls the house at night,
21 getting into everything. My parents have found a way to
22 sleep through her shenanigans. They shut their door so she
23 can't get in. I tried that too and she clawed at my door all
24 night, scratching deep down into the wood. I got in trouble
25 for that, too!
26   I keep telling myself that she'll calm down when she
27 gets older. But how many years will that take? Are cat years
28 like dog years? In cat years how old does she have to be? I

1   don't think I can survive much more. I haven't slept in
2   months.
3   I know one thing: The next time my parents tell me that
4   having a pet isn't as easy as it looks, I'll believe them! I may
5   never own another pet again.
6   *(Pause)* **Although** ... my friend Karli has a cute little fluffy
7   dog ... that seems pretty easy ...

9. Cartoons Aren't Just for Kids

(Girl or Guy)

1   I have a secret that I can never tell my friends. It's so
2 embarrassing that if they found out I would never be able to
3 live it down. I'd be the butt of jokes until the day I die.
4 Maybe even after. I'd probably be that kid that they talk
5 about year after year in school. Like, "Did you hear about
6 Eric Masters ... "

7   It doesn't help that I run with a rough crowd — rougher
8 than average at least. Not gang rough or anything, but some
9 of my friends have been suspended for one reason or
10 another and all of them have had either lunch detention or
11 Saturday detention. We're kind of the rebels of the school.
12 The rowdy ones. I'm not really proud of it, but it's important
13 that you understand the kind of guys I hang with so that you
14 can understand the severity of my problem. The reason why
15 I have to guard my secret from them. They would never get
16 it.

17   But maybe I'm just being paranoid. Or making a
18 mountain out of a molehill, like my grandpa would say.
19 Maybe it's really not that big of a deal. Maybe some of them
20 do it, too. Maybe I should just invite them over and lay it all
21 out on the table. Wouldn't that be funny, if after all this time
22 of worrying about it, they were doing it, too?

23   I guess I could take the chance. Put some snacks out,
24 all our favorites, and then take the plunge. Turn on the DVD
25 player and see what happens. Would they kick me out of the
26 group when, instead of a gory, blood-filled movie, a cute

1 furry cartoon character fills the screen? I mean, other guys
2 watch animated movies, don't they? They're just so funny.
3 And the music is awesome! It's really nothing to be
4 ashamed of, is it? Oh, who am I kidding? They'll think I'm
5 a freak! This is one secret I *must* keep.

10. Bieber Fever

(Guy)

1   OK! OK! I admit it. Does it make me any less of a boy?
2   No! It's not like I think the kid is cute or anything. He has
3   some really great songs out. Maybe if I just say it out loud,
4   I'll feel better. Don't judge me though, it is a seriously
5   contagious illness. OK, are you ready? Here goes: I have
6   *Bieber fever!*
7   See, it all started with my sister; clearly she is the one
8   to blame for this whole mess. She is like a super fan. She
9   has all the T-shirts, hats, posters, and his movie. She even
10   has his sunglasses. She was playing his album like nonstop,
11   and at first it was just annoying, but after a while I just got
12   used to it. Then the worst happened, my mom had the idea
13   that my sister and I don't spend enough time together so
14   she surprised us with concert tickets.
15   So there I was trapped, surrounded by the music that I
16   so desperately wanted to hate. But after hearing these
17   songs day and night, with the lyrics implanted in my head,
18   I started to sing along. I hated myself for doing this, but I
19   couldn't help it! The music became intoxicating. I was
20   singing, clapping, and having a great time at the concert. To
21   be honest, it all happened so fast, I was completely caught
22   off guard.
23   But here's the really embarrassing part: After the
24   concert, the fever continued, spreading quickly, and the only
25   medicine was to listen more. I was obsessed! If my friends
26   ever caught me listening to this, do you know how they
27   would make me suffer? I'd be ridiculed beyond belief. But
28   you know what? I'm not afraid to admit it anymore. It's not

1   who I am. It doesn't define me. In fact, it doesn't change
2   anything about me.
3   So I'm not ashamed of it anymore. That's right: *I have*
4   *Bieber fever!*

11. Holey Moley

(Guy)

1   I don't know how many times I've had to say this, but
2   here it goes again: This is a *mole,* not a pimple! Yeah, I
3   *know* it looks like a pimple and the fact that it's right here
4   on my chin where most pimples like to be and it's pink like
5   a pimple and even the size of a pimple, but I swear this
6   sucker is *not* a pimple. You know that stupid saying that "if
7   it looks like a rose and smells like a rose, then it's a rose"?
8   Well, that's just bull! Because even though this looks like a
9   pimple and all that, it's *not a pimple!*
10   I can prove it, too. Look at these pictures. Do you really
11   think that I'd have the *same* pimple in every school picture?
12   Year after year I just happen to break out in the same exact
13   spot? Does that even sound reasonable? Of course not! No
14   one has the same pimple month after month, year after
15   year.
16   It makes me want to wear a bandage on the stupid
17   thing. But then people would stare even more. If that's even
18   possible. It's like no one's ever seen a mole before. Well,
19   maybe they should meet my Aunt Edna. She's got a ton —
20   and half of them have little black hairs sticking out of them.
21   Disgusting! Maybe *that* would prove this isn't a zit, if I just
22   had hair sprouting from the top. But ewwww! That's even
23   more disgusting that a pimple. There's no winning is there?
24   I might as well just have an arrow painted on my face
25   pointing straight to it for the unobservant souls who haven't
26   noticed it yet. If there are any of those left! Which I doubt.
27   Even Mr. Jensen, who can't see his hand in front of his face,
28   has noticed it. And his glasses are so thick, they look like

1   bulletproof glass.
2   If only I were a girl, I could at least pass it off like Marilyn
3   Monroe did. But no one wants to see this on a guy. I guess
4   the good news is, if I ever get it removed, I'll have a cool
5   scar. At least girls dig scars, right?

12. Mower Envy

(Guy)

1 　　My father is ridiculous. In so many ways. But this last
2 thing is the most ridiculous thing I've ever heard of! He sold
3 our mower. Our nice John Deere riding mower that could
4 turn on a dime. I'm talking no effort mowing. It was a dream
5 to have mowing as my chore. I didn't even complain ... most
6 of the time.

7 　　And a riding mower is completely necessary for our yard,
8 I might add. No one mows over an acre by hand. Especially
9 not with our hills. They're like mini-mountains.

10 　　But even a self-propelled mower would be something I
11 could live with. Want to know what he got instead? This
12 antique-looking mower that doesn't even have a motor. I
13 didn't even know you could still find one of those. Didn't
14 they go out in like the 1800s or something? But this thing
15 is brand new. Shiny like a polished penny. That means some
16 idiot company is *still* making these things.

17 　　You probably think my dad is out to get me or punishing
18 me for some terrible injustice. But he isn't! He says, "We're
19 going green, son!" "Saving the planet" and all that jazz.
20 And he just had to throw in that I would be sure to build
21 muscles pushing that thing around our yard. He actually
22 had the nerve to make it sound like he was doing this for
23 me. "Won't hurt with the girls." Wink. Wink.

24 　　Well maybe so, except do you know how long it takes to
25 mow a yard with a sickle-blade mower? I might as well do it
26 with a pair of scissors! Maybe I can get my sister to trade
27 chores with me. She's the one with the muscles anyway.

13. Broccoli Is Not My BFF

(Girl or Guy)

1   Every morning since I can remember, my mother — the
2 one who is supposed to love me more than anything — has
3 given me a nasty baby poop-green-colored veggie shake to
4 make sure that I grow big and strong. Well, I'm done. I've
5 decided I don't want to be big and strong. There's
6 absolutely nothing wrong with small and weak. I'll be smart.
7 A super geek. Whatever. Besides, if that nasty broccoli,
8 celery, and seaweed — and who knows what else —
9 concoction hasn't made me "big and strong" by now, I don't
10 think it's going to.
11   Everyone I know gets cool stuff for breakfast. Cereal.
12 Donuts. Pancakes. Waffles. Pastries. Whoever said a drink
13 was a meal anyway? I want something I can chew — and not
14 just the occasional chunk of broccoli that didn't get blended
15 or pureed or pulverized into oblivion.
16   Enough! I want a breakfast I can sink my teeth into.
17 Something greasy like sausage and bacon. With an egg.
18 And cheese! And I want it on white bread. Maybe even a big
19 fat biscuit. Nothing whole wheat or whole grain or organic.
20 Just a normal greasy, buttery biscuit! With those peel off
21 layers so I can put butter in between every piece! Oh my
22 gosh. I'm drooling just thinking about it!
23   I just can't wait for tomorrow morning. That's the day I
24 take a stand. No more pureed baby poop gunk for me. Bring
25 on the grease.

14. Family Reunion = Family Drama

(Girl or Guy)

1   My mother is in a tizzy. Full tilt, one-hundred-miles-a-
2 minute frantic. The I-have-to-do-everything-this-second kind
3 of tizzy. It happens every year at this time. You'd think she'd
4 learn. You'd think we'd *all* learn. Maybe even leave town.
5 Plan a vacation or something. I know I would if I could. In
6 fact, I *will* as soon as I'm old enough to avoid all this chaos
7 and drama.

8   It's family reunion time. Which doesn't sound like a bad
9 thing, but believe me, it is. Not only does my grandma fly in
10 from Florida, but all my aunts and uncles and all the
11 cousins come, too. I think there's like seventy-five of us all
12 together. My mom goes all out. Plans the menu and a bunch
13 of games for the family to play. It's like a mini Olympics
14 kind of thing. Family against family. And everything has to
15 be perfect. To the T. And to be honest, it all *is* perfect: the
16 house, the food, the decorations, the games. All of it. Until
17 everyone gets here.

18   It happens every time. One aunt will say something
19 nasty to one uncle or vice versa and then another aunt or
20 uncle will hear about it and choose a side. Within no time
21 the group is split into two. On really bad years, it's split into
22 even more factions.

23   People start yelling. Then people start crying. Then they
24 start hugging. Eventually they start laughing. Like nothing
25 ever happened. It's a crazy rollercoaster ride of emotions.
26 It's the same thing every year. Why would anyone want to

1   be a part of that?! I know I don't. But every year they all
2   come back. And mom gets in a tizzy. And tells everyone it's
3   no big deal. That it's all worth it ...
4   Completely insane! I'm starting to think that we need to
5   add a psychiatrist to the guest list. My family needs some
6   serious therapy!

15. Ow, That Burns!

(Girl)

1   Here's a piece of advice for you: When the directions say
2   to try the product out on a test area before applying to a
3   large section, you really should listen.
4   My legs are burning so bad. I feel like a million bees have
5   stung me. Why did I ever listen to Molly about hair removal
6   cream? Nothing — not even legs as smooth as hers — is
7   worth this kind of torture!
8   I should've just waited for Mom to let me get a razor.
9   Even though her rule about being thirteen before you can
10   shave is about as antiquated as the *electric* razor she wants
11   to give me. I've had hairy legs for years already. What girl
12   waits until they're thirteen these days? Just because my
13   grandmother made her wait until that age doesn't mean she
14   has to punish me that way, too.
15   Couldn't she see what an ape I was turning into?
16   Apparently the hair on my legs didn't know it was supposed
17   to wait until I was older. If I waited much longer, I would've
18   looked like I was wearing a sweater on my legs.
19   But even still, nothing is worth this pain. Now I look like
20   I was sunbathing about ten feet from the sun. My legs are
21   beet red. And they hurt to even touch them. I can't even put
22   lotion on them — it hurts too much!
23   I'll never do this again, I guarantee you that! I don't care
24   if I have to wear pants for the rest of my life. But right now,
25   I can't even do that. No way am I letting pants anywhere
26   near these firecracker legs. I don't know what I'm going to
27   wear to school tomorrow. Maybe Mom has one of those
28   skirts that goes all the way to the floor. She seems to like
29   living in the past so much.

16. Biking — It's for Kids

(Girl or Guy)

1   My parents are acting like a couple of twelve-year-olds.
2 They have become obsessed with biking. They bought new
3 bikes, new helmets, all the gadgets right down to two new
4 thermal water bottles. My dad even bought these black
5 spandex pants with padding built in. They look ridiculous on
6 him. He's walking around with a built-in butt. And believe
7 me, my father does *not* need extra padding in that area.
8   It's *all* they ever talk about now. "This would've been a
9 good day for biking." "Oh, we could've biked here, instead
10 of driving." It's nonstop. But that's not all. Now they want
11 to involve *me*. Our whole week of family vacation is all about
12 biking. Get this! We're going to the beach, but not to lay out
13 and catch some rays, or splash in the ocean, or build a
14 sandcastle. Oh no! We're going to the beach to go *biking!*
15 Every day either on an island trail or down the beach. I
16 didn't even know you could bike on a beach. Who in their
17 right mind *wants* to? It's a beach for Pete's sake. A place to
18 relax. Chill out. Enjoy the quiet.
19   Shouldn't they have outgrown the desire to bike, like
20 twenty or thirty years ago? I don't even like to bike and I'm
21 supposed to. But maybe I would if I wasn't hearing about it
22 all the time. I actually heard them discussing selling our car
23 and only biking everywhere. They've completely gone
24 insane! Who wants to bike when it's cold or raining? How
25 many groceries can you fit on a bike? Have they even
26 thought of these things? And if they sell the car, what am I
27 going to drive when I turn sixteen?! It won't be a bike, I can
28 promise you that.

17. Eighteen = Forever

(Guy)

1   A few stupid kids should not ruin things for everyone.
2 They were the ones that broke the law. They were the ones
3 that drove over one hundred miles an hour down a curvy
4 country road without seatbelts. They were the ones that lost
5 control. Not me. Not my friends. Not the kids I know. It's so
6 unfair. It's not that I don't feel bad about what happened. I
7 do. Who wouldn't? Young lives cut short is tragic no matter
8 how it happens.

9   But now they want to change the legal driving age to
10 eighteen. *Eighteen!* That's insane! I will be graduated from
11 high school before then. That means I will have to ride the
12 bus every day of school even through my senior year. And
13 that my parents will have to drive me to *both* of my proms.
14 Can you imagine how awful that would be?

15   And I can forget about getting a job after school
16 because I won't have a way to get there. Both my parents
17 work full-time. They can't cart me back and forth to a job.
18 And no job means no money. No money means no dating
19 and no car for the day when I can drive.

20   How can they even propose something so ridiculous?
21 Have they even thought about the consequences of such a
22 law? A knee-jerk reaction to anything is *never* good. Don't
23 those educated lawmakers understand that? Do they need
24 to be schooled by a bunch of outraged teenagers? Don't
25 punish the whole because of the actions of a few.

26   If I have to wait six more years, instead of the three I've
27 been counting on, I'll die! *(Pause)* No. I know what I'll do. I'll
28 drive illegally. That's what I'll do. And I'll get all my friends

1   to do it, too. Then those stupid lawmakers will see how
2   crazy it was to take away our freedom! We'll show them
3   irresponsible. And reckless. And out of control. You just
4   wait and see.

18. The One and Only

(Girl or Guy)

1   I know it's been said that some kids ask their parents
2 for a brother or a sister. At least that's what adults say.
3 Personally, I don't believe that any sane kid who's an only
4 child would ever be dumb enough to actually *ask* for a
5 sibling. Why would they? They have everything! They *get*
6 everything. Who would mess up that kind of gig?
7   If someone really does, and again, I highly doubt the
8 stories are true, it could only be after extreme brainwashing
9 of the eager parents who just can't wait to grow their
10 family. They are the culprits! I'm telling you this straight.
11 They know they have to sell that little-bundle-of-joy scam to
12 you because you would never come up with that on your
13 own.
14   Another kid means less of everything for you.
15   Less space. Less toys. Less attention. Less *everything.*
16   And then, if you're really unlucky and the new brother or
17 sister is better than you — you know what I mean: cuter,
18 smarter, better behaved, more athletic, whatever the case
19 may be — you might as well just fade into the background
20 because your position of first and foremost will be
21 relinquished forever.
22   Now they'll try to sell you on the joys of having someone
23 to play with, a "forever friend," but don't buy it! Think about
24 it. How many friends do you have with brothers and/or
25 sisters? Do you *ever* see them together? Happy? Do they
26 even seem to *like* each other?
27   Yeah, my little brother over there, he's cute and all.
28 Right now. When all he does is sleep, eat, poop, and cry.

1   But by the time he's old enough to actually "play with me,"
2   I'll be moving out for college. I'm telling you, it's a scam!
3   Don't buy into it. Being an only child is amazing.

19. Too Old to Say "I Do"

(Girl)

1   My great aunt Lou is seventy-seven years old. And she's
2 awesome. She still drives a car. Likes to ride her bike around
3 her neighborhood. She still works full-time. The old lady
4 doesn't quit! And not too long ago, she went skydiving. So
5 it's easy to see that she acts *way* younger than she really is.
6 And I'm all for that ... except for this latest thing of hers.
7   She's getting married. Again. After thirty years of living
8 alone, she's found the second perfect man for her and is
9 going to say "I do." At her age, that's just gross. They even
10 hold hands and kiss and stuff. Now who wants to watch two
11 wrinkled old people swap spit? Not me! That's for sure. I
12 mean I'd be OK with the whole love and wedding thing if they
13 would just act their age.
14   But really, what's the point? Part of marriage is growing
15 old together, but they're already old! Can't they just be
16 friends? Why do the whole shebang? White dress, flowers,
17 altar? Doesn't that seem a little overdramatic? What if one of
18 them keels over from all of the excitement? How would they
19 explain that to their two hundred plus guests?
20   I'm not anti-love. I promise. And I love my great aunt
21 Lou. I just think she's too old to be acting like a lovesick
22 teenager. She's supposed to be planning her retirement, not
23 a wedding. But I guess Lou doesn't care about age one little
24 bit because I just heard Mom on the phone and guess who
25 they want to be the flower girl? Me. Doesn't she know I'm
26 twelve years old? That's way past the flower girl age limit!
27 This just proves that Aunt Lou does *not* need to be getting
28 married because clearly she has *lost her mind!*

20. Beach Bum Brother

(Guy)

1   This is the life! The sun beating down on my back. The
2 ocean lulling me into the most peaceful feeling I've ever
3 known. Not to mention the view — and I'm not talking about
4 the ocean! Look at all the girls! And look how they're
5 dressed. Or should I say *not* dressed?! I've never seen
6 bikinis so skimpy. No wonder my sister says that mom
7 makes her dress like a grandma. She would never be
8 allowed out in public in something like that.
9   They're practically naked! Those little triangles aren't
10 big enough to be an eye patch, much less a piece of actual
11 clothing. I don't think I can thank my parents enough for
12 bringing me to the beach on vacation. It's like my own little
13 slice of heaven. Tan skin everywhere. I could stay here
14 forever. Live on the beach. Become a surfer maybe. Why
15 not? I could be a pro surfer one day. No one says a guy from
16 Kentucky can't surf. I'd just need some lessons and a little
17 bit of practice. And I would practice — day and night!
18   *(Pause)* Well, OK. Maybe not night. I don't want to be
19 shark bait or anything. Besides, how would I see all the hot
20 chicks in the dark?
21   Look! Here comes one now. Her long hair flowing in the
22 wind. Long tan legs. I think she's coming toward me *(Squint*
23 *and put hand to eyes)* ... darn sun ...
24   *(Cover eyes.)* Oh my gosh! *Gross!* That's my sister!
25 Mom, quick! Get Ashley a towel!

21. Take a Seat

(Guy)

1   Riding the bus to school is the most humiliating
2 experience of any kid's life. Doesn't matter who you are,
3 how old you are, or how cool you think you are, there's
4 always someone who makes you feel about an inch tall at
5 some point in your bus riding career.
6   You step on. Trying to look natural, uncaring as to where
7 you're going to sit, while the whole time you're scanning,
8 searching for the perfect spot. The empty seat that you can
9 actually sit in. Not the pseudo-empty seat that you *think*
10 you can sit in and then much to your embarrassment, a leg
11 or an arm is thrown across it and the dreaded word "saved"
12 comes out of someone's mouth. Even though saving seats
13 is not technically allowed on the bus.
14   It's hard to recover from that one. Hard to look
15 unaffected as you move to the next empty spot. Two
16 "saved" in a row and you might as well hang your head in
17 shame and sit with the kid who everyone knows eats
18 boogers.
19   The worst part of all is the driver yelling, "Take a seat,"
20 like it's an easy task and you're a moron who can't seem to
21 do it. Has Mr. Glass completely forgotten the dynamics of
22 bus riding? "Taking a seat" is a process that can't be
23 rushed or you're sure to face rejection and embarrassment.
24 You have to pick just right and then pray that when you do
25 sit down and put your back to the rest of the bus that no
26 one decides to throw something at your head.
27   That happened to me last year — raw egg, right between
28 my shoulder blades. Right above my collar so that egg

1   dripped all down my back. Smelled like a rotten egg all day
2   in school.
3   So Mr. Glass can just hold his horses. I'll "take a seat"
4   when I'm good and ready.

22. Ban on Homework

(Girl or Guy)

1   I just heard the most amazing news! I never thought my
2 mom being on the school board could be a good thing, but
3 because of her, I just got the biggest scoop ever.
4   Get this. They're thinking about banning homework. Can
5 you believe that? I thought my mom was just trying to
6 prank me last night when she told us that at dinner, but my
7 friend Heather just heard it, too! They're going to vote on it
8 at next month's meeting after they hold a debate over the
9 pros and cons.
10   Hello? What can possibly be the cons? Everything is a
11 pro! No more late nights doing page after page of math
12 problems that I'll never need to know in real life. No more
13 projects that take all weekend to complete. No more
14 summer reading projects that completely ruin the whole
15 entire summer. Even if they don't take that long to really do,
16 they're hanging over your head the whole time. It's like this
17 huge weight on your shoulders. Who can enjoy summer like
18 that? Weighted down with stress and worry. We're supposed
19 to be having fun! Living it up. If I wanted to work all
20 summer, I'd get a job. A paying one. Not reading some
21 stupid thick book that I would never ever pick to read on my
22 own, and then making some lame collage or shadow box
23 about it.
24   Clearly I'm all for a homework ban. I say, "Free the
25 nights! Free the summers!" Let us have some time off.
26 "Free our brains!" That can be the slogan. I'll go tell Mom.
27 I'll make her a sign. She can hold it up at next month's
28 meeting. She can be the one to start the revolution. She'll

1   be the coolest mom ever!

2   *(Mime picking up a piece of paper)* **Wait! What's this? Pro**

3   **homework? Are you kidding me? Mom! We need to talk!**

23. Always a Follower

(Girl)

1   You know that saying, "Always a follower, never a
2   leader?" Well, I think that's me. I "follow" so many people on
3   the Internet that I can't live my own life. I'm too busy reading
4   about every little thing everyone else does. That's all I do. I
5   guess you could say that I'm addicted to being nosy.

6   Why should it matter to me if Brad gets a triple chocolate
7   latte with extra cream? Or that Mandy just "checked in" at
8   Star Spa to get her mani-pedi? I'm a follower of nine hundred
9   and eighty-three people! That's nine hundred and eighty-
10 three updates I get every day. And most people update
11 several times a day so I'm guessing that I get over five
12 thousand in twenty-four hours.

13 It's no wonder my grades are dropping. Who has time for
14 homework and studying? I have to keep up with what's going
15 on. Who's dating who. Who's dumping who. And I don't even
16 know all these people. At least not personally.

17 Sure I have some real friends that I follow. But for some
18 reason it's not near as exciting to know that my friend is
19 getting a haircut as it is to know the inner workings of my
20 favorite celebrities. Who knew they do and like a lot of the
21 same things that I do? It's like I *know* them now. They're
22 real people. Doing real things. Day in and day out. Like me.

23 *(Pause)* Only I'm not really doing anything anymore ... not
24 really ... maybe I should quit ... but then how would I know
25 if Selena and Justin stay together — or better yet, if they
26 break up? I'd be in the dark. Clueless.

27 Maybe I'll just trim my list down. I don't really need to
28 follow my friends on there ... I can see them in school ...
29 *(Walk off)*

24. Mom's Dirty Little Secret

(Girl or Guy)

1   I think my mom has a problem. Scratch that. I *know* my
2 mom has a problem. A real bad drinking problem. It all
3 started about three years ago when my dad got transferred
4 to Michigan and my mom decided we wouldn't go.
5 Apparently she loves the sun and warm weather here in
6 Florida more than she loves my dad. She said she wouldn't
7 move north until you-know-what freezes over.
8   My dad tried to make it work for awhile. Came home
9 about once every three months or so. But they've been
10 getting farther and farther apart now. I think it's been about
11 a year now ... who am I kidding? I *know* exactly how long
12 it's been. The last time I saw my dad was on my birthday.
13 Last year. Thirteen months ago. I guess that was his
14 present to me. Coming to visit. Guess he didn't feel the
15 need to do it again this year. It's not that I blame him. It is
16 a long drive and we aren't rich enough for him to fly. And
17 mom hasn't made the trip up there once. Not even in the
18 summer when Michigan would feel great compared to here.
19   She's just stubborn. And drunk. Most of the time. I
20 don't even know why we can't live in Michigan anyway. It's
21 not like she ever leaves the house. Just groceries and liquor
22 store. Can't she do that up north just as well? At least then
23 I'd get to see my dad. And we'd be a family again. If she's
24 so miserable that she has to drink all the time, why did she
25 make us stay?
26   Next time my dad comes to visit, I'm going back with

1   him. I don't mind the cold and snow one little bit. I think it'd
2   be great to actually build a snowman or go sledding. Dad
3   and I could even have a snowball fight.
4   So what if he missed my birthday ... I'm sure he'll be
5   home for Christmas.

25. Beat Her to the Punch

(Guy)

1   See that girl over there? The cute one with the short
2 blonde hair and the skinny jeans on? Well, that is the girl of
3 my dreams. Allie. The girl I've liked since kindergarten. And
4 I'm lucky to say that she is also my girlfriend. Has been for
5 three weeks now. Three short wonderful weeks. The best
6 weeks of my whole life.
7   I can't believe it has to end. But it does. Last class I
8 asked Jenny from social studies to go with me. And she said
9 yes. That's right, I'm now officially cheating on the girl of my
10 dreams. The girl I would never ever in a million years cheat
11 on. Are you confused? Well so am I! We're all on the same
12 page now. Blindsided. Dumbfounded.
13   See, my friend Percy said he heard Allie tell her best
14 friend that she's going to dump me at the rally later this
15 afternoon. I don't even know why! Things are going great. We
16 haven't even had our first fight. Why would she want to break
17 up with me? I haven't done anything wrong.
18   That's why I took Percy's advice and asked Jenny out. I
19 didn't want the whole school feeling sorry for me. Thinking
20 that I'm the loser that got dumped. Percy said I should dump
21 Allie first and have a backup all ready to go. So now when
22 she goes to break up with me, I'll tell her all about Jenny!
23   *(Pause and look to side)* What? Are you joking? Allie didn't
24 really say that? She really isn't going to break up with me?
25 This isn't funny, Percy. What am I going to do about Jenny?
26 When Allie hears about this, she really *will* dump me! *(Look*
27 *to side again)* Hey! Who are you texting? Is that *Allie's*
28 *number?* You planned this all along? You're totally going to
29 steal the girl of my dreams!

26. What's Next? Perms?

(Girl)

1   So if I tied a twig in my hair, do you think people would
2 copy that? Or maybe a string of pearls. Or a shoestring. Or
3 something else completely lame and stupid. Can't these
4 girls see how ridiculous they look with a feather in their hair?
5 We're not birds! There is no reason a feather should be
6 stuck on our heads. They think they look so cool, too.
7 Strutting around like a peacock, thinking they're the fashion
8 setters of the school. Trendsetters. Ha! They didn't come up
9 with the idea — they just copied it from one of those stupid
10 magazines they're always pawing all over.

11   Just like last year when they all wore their shirts inside
12 out with the tags sticking up so everyone could see where
13 they shopped and what size they wore. They're just a bunch
14 of posers. Haven't they ever heard my mother's favorite
15 phrase, "If everyone was jumping off the bridge, would
16 you?" They can't even think for themselves. I don't think
17 there is anything they wouldn't copy. I bet if that magazine
18 said perms were back in style that every single one of those
19 straight-haired girls would show up looking like a clown.
20 With a curly old fro.

21   Or maybe a big wall of bangs will come back in style. I
22 would love to see Miranda sporting a look like that. She
23 hasn't had bangs since she was a baby. I know because we
24 *used* to be friends. Back before she started buying into this
25 fashion baloney. Back when we used to laugh at girls that
26 copied their looks right out of a magazine. Back when she
27 never, ever would've put a feather in her hair.

28   But I guess it's appropriate since they really are kind of
29 like birds since they all *flock* together.

27. The QB with the BO

(Girl)

1   I finally got the boy of my dreams. The guy I've had my
2 eye on since I started middle school. He's so cute. And tall.
3 A good six inches taller than me, which is almost
4 impossible since I'm the tallest girl in the eighth grade.
5 Every boyfriend I've had has been shorter than me by about
6 a foot. I finally get to look up when I'm talking to my
7 boyfriend! It's awesome.
8   He's perfect in every way, too. QB of the football team
9 and plays pretty good, probably the best on the team. I can
10 totally see us being a couple all through this year and into
11 high school. We'd be the couple that everyone talks about.
12 The couple that beats the odds and ends up getting married
13 after college.
14   Well, I could totally see that except for one little thing. I
15 can't stand to be around him. He's so sweet and nice and
16 funny ... but ... he smells! Real bad. Believe me, if it was
17 just a little odor, I'd suffer through it. But his isn't the kind
18 of smell you can endure on a daily basis. This is the kind of
19 smell that gets stuck in your nostrils and won't get out. It's
20 worse than when I forget to clean out the litter box. It's
21 worse than when my brother stinks up the bathroom. It's
22 even worse than when I left my egg salad sandwich in my
23 backpack for three weeks over Christmas break ... OK ...
24 maybe it isn't worse than *that*. But this is daily exposure.
25 Not a one time, throw-your-backpack-in-the-dumpster kind
26 of thing!
27   I thought I could develop an immunity to it, but I can't.
28 If anything, I think I'm getting *more* sensitive to it. I swear I

1   can smell him coming down the hall. So there's really no
2   choice. I have to do it. The QB with the BO has got to G-O!

28. There's No Such Thing as Love

(Girl)

1   I'll never believe in love again. Ever. For as long as I live.
2 I've given up hope. The whole idea of love is completely
3 ruined for me. If the two most perfect people in the world
4 can't make it work, how can anyone else even have a
5 chance to stay in love?
6   I've been watching these two celebrities since the
7 moment they fell in love. And I'm not the only one. The
8 whole world was sucked into how perfect everything was for
9 them. We watched them date, get engaged, get married, and
10 have kids. How can they possibly split up now? Their
11 children are still young. One is still in diapers. They can't do
12 that to them. To us!
13   Clearly they haven't tried hard enough. One, or maybe
14 both, gave up too easily. Why isn't he fighting to keep her?
15 Or why isn't she trying to keep him? Can't they see how
16 perfect their little family is? How can they possibly destroy
17 it? Throw it all away and leave their lives and the whole
18 world in shambles?
19   I don't even know who to be mad at. The news stories
20 aren't giving me much to go on. Whose fault is it? I can't
21 even imagine that one of them is a cheater. They can't be.
22 They could never do that to one another. Besides, neither
23 one of them could find anyone better because they are the
24 best of the best.
25   It has to be someone else's fault. Like maybe one of
26 them has a horrible mother. Certainly a bad mother-in-law

1   could destroy a perfectly happy marriage. Or maybe this is
2   all just a publicity stunt. They're only acting like they are
3   splitting up to get media attention ... or maybe it's the
4   media's fault. That's it! They've been hounded all these
5   years by the paparazzi. Never having a moment's peace.
6   Never being able to be a family in private. That's got to be
7   it. They didn't do anything wrong. How could they? It was
8   us. We did this. We, the nosiest people in the world, have
9   destroyed the most perfect family ever! Worse yet, we have
10 destroyed *love!*

29. PE Should Be Optional

(Guy)

1   PE is a joke. At least it is for people like me. People who
2 are perfectly content to never ever know if they can run a
3 mile, or do one hundred sit-ups, or be the last one out in
4 dodgeball. Of course it's absolutely perfect for the kind of
5 guys who like to show off their mad basketball or tennis
6 skills. Get the girls' attention by running a few hurdles.
7   Why can't art class be mandatory instead? A class
8 where I actually could look good. I could actually show the
9 girls a thing or two about shading and three-dimensional
10 drawing. And I wouldn't even break a sweat and smell all
11 nasty like the stupid jock boys. Guys like me know how to
12 treat a girl. How to pay attention to them and listen. Jock
13 guys only know how to pay attention to themselves. I swear
14 they spend more time in the mirror in the bathroom after
15 class than I think the girls do. How can girls even find that
16 attractive? Smug *and* smelly. Gross!
17   If the school would just eliminate gym class, the other
18 guys like me — the non-jocks — might have a shot at
19 getting a girlfriend. It would level the playing field a little.
20 Give us an opportunity to shine. Of course it would really
21 help if they would just ban sports altogether. Now that
22 would be a real dream. Just think how much money is spent
23 on uniforms and equipment. Money that could be spent on
24 new computers or art supplies. Banning sports could be the
25 greatest thing to ever happen to the school system.
26   Why am I the only one who sees how unfair it is to force
27 a guy like me into gym shorts and put him on display for
28 everyone to see? My pale legs weren't meant for the public!

1   I can barely stand them in private.
2   Oh well, here goes another forty-five minutes of pure
3   torture.

30. Buy the Boxes

(Girl)

1 My mother thinks she's funny. A real impromptu
2 comedian. Every time we go to the shoe store it's the same
3 old joke. "Why don't you just get the boxes?" she says.
4 Every stinking time. And then she laughs like it's the first
5 time she's ever said it.
6   I get it. OK?! My feet are big. Big enough that the boxes
7 would actually fit better than the actual shoes. Haha. *So*
8 funny. Might even be a good thing, if I was a guy. Which I'm
9 not. I'm a considerably short girl with *big* feet. Not a tall girl
10 who it might actually be socially acceptable for her to have
11 overly large feet.
12   I am completely out of proportion. My feet are bigger
13 than my father's. Not kidding. He has actually borrowed my
14 sneakers before and then complained because they were too
15 big. Again, might not be so bad if my dad had extremely
16 small feet for a man. But my dad's a whopping six foot three
17 inches and has the feet that actually match that size.
18   So why are my feet of Amazon proportion? Who the heck
19 knows? The doctor sure doesn't. In fact, the doctor doesn't
20 even seem the least bit concerned that my feet are gigantic.
21 Which proves that we probably need to find a new doctor
22 because clearly I am some kind of genetic abnormality. A
23 genetic freak that needs to be poked and prodded until
24 some kind of treatment can be found. They can't just
25 expect me to stomp around in these giant feet for the rest
26 of my life, can they?
27   I'm serious. If they grow any more, I *will* have to buy the
28 boxes instead of the shoes. Then we'll see how funny that
29 really is, won't we, Mom?

31. Drill Sergeant Father

(Girl or Guy)

1   My father is all about "the rules." He has a rule for
2   absolutely everything. And I mean *everything*. You think I'm
3   kidding? Listen to this.
4   Television watching: no more than two hours per night.
5   One of which must be educational in some manner. Must sit
6   at least three feet from the television set and have the
7   volume no louder than the mid mark. Commercials are to be
8   muted so as not to convince me to buy or want something
9   that I don't really need.
10   Afterschool snacks: may choose one of three options.
11 Mini carrots with *no* dip, sliced apples with low fat caramel
12 sauce, or one small bowl of air popped popcorn. Not the
13 entire bag. I repeat, *not* the entire bag. Snack must be
14 consumed between three and four o'clock so as not to spoil
15 dinner and must be cleaned up immediately. One single
16 crumb detected means vacuum duty for the whole month.
17   Homework: must be done immediately after school. No
18 exceptions. Even on Fridays when you have the whole
19 weekend to do it. Must be completed before dinner time. If
20 not, no television for rest of the night, even if the homework
21 is completed long before bedtime.
22   Speaking of bedtime: lights out at ten o'clock. No
23 exceptions. Even on the weekends. Even during a sleepover.
24 Even during holidays and snow days and parent-teacher no
25 school days. And lights out is preceded by thirty minutes of
26 reading. Not a book of your choice. A book that my father
27 chooses. When finished, an oral report must be presented at
28 dinner, outlining characters and a summary of the plot. An

1   incomplete book report means having to read the entire
2   book over again and doing a written follow-up report.
3   Now do you believe me? My father is a drill sergeant!
4   And those aren't even half the rules. I swear we even have
5   posted rules on how to brush our teeth. And take a shower.
6   And make our beds. We have rules for the rules. I
7   understand that my dad spent a lot of time in the military,
8   but this is ridiculous!

32. Clipped and Chopped

(Girl)

1   My friend Brittany always has the cutest hair. And
2 makeup. And clothes. And nails. She's the perfect package
3 really. It's easy to see why she would want to be a
4 beautician one day because she is so good at all of it.
5   That's why when she offered to cut my hair for me, I
6 didn't even think twice. A free haircut from someone who
7 looks so great? Why not? She even had professional
8 haircutting scissors and a magazine of hairstyles that I
9 could pick from. Besides, I was ready to chop it all off
10 anyway. After two back-to-back dying sessions, my hair was
11 completely frazzled. All woolly and frizzy. I couldn't even
12 stand touching it!
13   But here's the thing: Looking like a beautician and *being*
14 a beautician are completely different things. She completely
15 chopped up my hair. I have more layers than a Pillsbury
16 biscuit! To even this out, I would have to practically shave
17 my head.
18   I had to spend my entire allowance on a set of hair
19 extensions. Yes, I bought human hair after just having a
20 head full of perfectly good ... well, OK, frizzy ... hair! I could
21 have bought the best conditioner in the world for the amount
22 of money I just spent on buying someone else's hair. I don't
23 even want to think about where they get all that hair — it's
24 not dead bodies, is it? That's just gross!
25   So I guess the moral of the story is: Just because
26 someone looks the part, doesn't mean they can *play* the
27 part. Sorry, Brit, but no more haircuts until *after* you go to
28 beauty school.

33. Mother Steals the Show

(Girl)

1   I know she didn't do it on purpose. At least that's what
2 I tell myself anyway. Sometimes I believe it and sometimes
3 I don't. Maybe if she didn't have a history of getting all the
4 attention *all* of the time, it would be easier to buy that the
5 whole thing really was a horrible accident. But with my mom
6 ... who knows? She definitely doesn't like sharing the
7 limelight. Not even with me, and I'm her daughter.
8   She really did go all out though. My thirteenth birthday
9 party had everything. A Seventies-themed party with cool
10 decorations. She even rented a disco ball for dancing and
11 transformed our basement into a real-looking discothèque!
12 Very impressive. My dad didn't even complain about how
13 much money she spent. But then how could he, when my
14 mom blows through that kind of money on herself all of the
15 time? She has so much jewelry that she had to have a
16 whole closet made to put it in.
17   But she was being a really good sport about it all. She
18 even spent a lot of time doing my hair and makeup and
19 bought me the perfect dress for my disco theme. I should've
20 known that all of that focus on me had to be driving her
21 crazy deep down inside. My father doesn't call her princess
22 for nothing. He's spoiled her rotten since the day they met.
23 Sometimes, I'm surprised she even wanted to have a child
24 because of losing some of the attention from my dad. Well,
25 at least in theory. It's not that my dad doesn't *try* to pay
26 attention to me, it's just that my mom has always sucked
27 it all up.
28   So am I surprised that at the exact moment that all eyes

1   were on me — the moment I was blowing out my thirteen
2   candles — my mother just happened to fall halfway down
3   the basement steps? Not in the least. The only real surprise
4   would be if she actually didn't do it on purpose. Bravo, Mom.
5   As always, you completely *stole* the show.

34. If I'm Here, I'm Here

(Girl or Guy)

1   I think college has it all right. Did you know that they
2 don't even take attendance in most schools? Teachers don't
3 care whether you show up or not. It's completely on you. If
4 you can skip class and still make good grades, why should
5 they care if you actually sit in a seat and listen to them
6 drone on and on? Some people, like me, do better on their
7 own. I can read the book by myself, thank you very much. I
8 don't need someone else telling me what to highlight,
9 what's important, and what I need to remember. I have a
10 photographic mind. I can remember it all!

11   So why can't all schools be this way? Sure would help
12 with those obnoxious kids who are forced to come to class
13 and then make everyone else's life miserable. My teacher
14 spends so much time yelling at the bad kids that the ones
15 who really do want to learn, like me, can't learn anyway.
16 We'd do much better on our own in a quiet setting where we
17 can think than in a rowdy classroom full of hooligans.

18   I wish I could take all of my classes online. Then I
19 wouldn't ever have to go to class and put up with all those
20 unnecessary distractions. If I could go at my own pace, I'd
21 probably have a four-point-oh GPA and finish school several
22 years early. I'd be in college in no time, away from these
23 losers who think reading the Cliffs Notes on a book is the
24 same thing as actually reading the book. Why should I be
25 subjected to this kind of ignorance?

26   Maybe I can talk my mom into homeschooling me. It's
27 the perfect solution. I'm sure she'd love spending more time
28 with me, and I'd love spending less time surrounded by

1 morons. Why didn't I think of this before now? It's going to
2 be just like college — no attendance required.

35. Miracle Mushroom

(Girl or Guy)

1   I don't see why my mom is freaking out. It's really not
2 that big of a deal. In fact when you stop and think about it,
3 it really is quite amazing. Like for real, who knew that a
4 mushroom could actually grow behind a toilet? Instead of
5 being so upset and ranting and raving about how dirty I
6 keep my bathroom, she should be impressed at the miracle
7 of it all. No sun. No nutrients. No dirt. That's a pretty
8 determined little mushroom if you ask me. We should be
9 studying it, not freaking out about it.
10 And now she's mad that I told my science teacher all
11 about the little miracle mushroom. But how could I not? It
12 was worth it just to see my teacher's face. I could tell she
13 didn't believe me. I had to show her the little fungi just to
14 prove to her I wasn't making it all up. Come on ... how could
15 anyone possibly make up a story like this? Who would even
16 think that it's possible? Sure, I know that mushrooms grow
17 in dark, damp places ... outside! Not in a bathroom.
18 Anyway, that cool little growth has caused a whole lot of
19 trouble for me. Now Mom is making me clean the bathroom
20 twice a week. That's completely ridiculous. No one does
21 that. And I'm not talking just a quick run through. She
22 wants the whole shebang: toilet, shower, sink, mirror, and
23 floors swept *and* mopped! But that's not all. She wants my
24 room picked up *every day!* Nothing allowed on the floors or
25 stuffed under my bed, or shoved in the closet. "Who knows
26 what could grow in here!" she said when she opened my
27 closet door.
28 Geez. Can you say, "drama queen"? One stupid tiny
29 mushroom and now we might as well sterilize the house.

36. Food Fight Fun

(Girl or Guy)

1   Want to know the absolute best food to have in a food
2   fight? Beets. You stick your straw in and it makes a perfect
3   pellet to shoot out at your friends or enemies. Another good
4   one is mashed potatoes. They launch great right off the
5   spoon and make an awesome splat when they hit the target.
6   Of course a food fight wouldn't be complete without ketchup
7   packets. You slam them just right and they can spurt out a
8   good ten feet! You just have to be careful that they don't get
9   you, too.
10   I love that my school hosts an annual free food fight day.
11   It's amazing to actually get to have a full-blown all-out food
12   war and not get grounded for life for it. We all wear old
13   clothes, shoes, hats — some even wear camouflage to make
14   it more like a war zone. Which it is! There is so much food
15   flying through the air, it's like that story where it's raining
16   meatballs out of the sky. It's the best thing ever. You don't
17   want it to end. What kid doesn't dream of having an all-out
18   food war?
19   But then just like all dreams, it has to end. And let me
20   tell you, cleaning up a food fight is not anywhere close to as
21   much fun as having a food fight. Do you have any idea how
22   hard it is to scrub ketchup out of the cracks in the tile? Or
23   mashed potatoes off the ceiling? The worst is the beet
24   juice. Man, that stuff stains! My hands get raw from
25   scrubbing so hard. We aren't allowed to leave one little
26   speck of food on anything. In fact, the cafeteria gets so
27   clean afterward, it sparkles like nothing I've ever seen. I'm
28   starting to wonder if that isn't the plan in the first place. It's

1   like the annual spring cleaning and we're the little worker
2   bees that do it ... but you know what? I don't even care. I
3   can't wait until next year! I'm bringing tomatoes.

37. Shopping Go-Cart

(Guy)

1   My brother and I are in big, big trouble. I wish I could
2 say it was all his fault, but the truth is, I was the brains
3 behind the stupid idea. And now we've got to confess
4 everything to Mom before things get really out of hand. Only
5 now I think it may be too late. Especially now that she's
6 called the cops. Which means I really should have told her
7 everything *before* she did that.

8   This is what happens when you leave two boys in the car
9 while you grocery shop and say you'll only be a few minutes
10 but then you're really gone for close to an hour. We were
11 good the first little bit so if she'd come out like she said,
12 none of this would've happened. Not that I'm trying to
13 blame Mom or anything, but you can see that in a way, it is
14 all her fault.

15   Anyway, after about fifteen minutes and changing the
16 radio station about a zillion times, I happened to notice the
17 cart return just a few spots down from us. It's not that I
18 haven't noticed them before but this time I started thinking
19 about how fun it would be for Harry, that's my brother, and
20 I to race them down the parking lot.

21   So we did. And that's when it happened. Harry bumped
22 into my cart and before I could stop, I slammed into our car.
23 The cart scraped down the side and left a huge dent! Luckily
24 no one saw us so we quickly put the carts back in the return
25 and then just as we were standing there looking at it, trying
26 to figure out what to do, Mom walked up. You should've
27 seen her face! She almost dropped her groceries, too. There
28 was no way I could tell her the truth. She loves her car.

1   I made up a lie about how this car sped through the
2 parking lot, swiping her car, and then driving off. She asked
3 me more and more questions and I made up more and more
4 lies. The type of car. The color. How old I thought it was.
5 What the driver looked like. Lie after lie! And now she's just
6 repeated all of that to the policeman on the phone. And now
7 he's on his way. I'm going to get arrested! Taken away in
8 handcuffs. Locked up in jail. All because of a stupid
9 shopping cart ride. Harry! Tell Mom that I love her ...

38. High School Anxiety

(Girl or Guy)

1   I don't think I'm ready for high school next year. I like
2 being in middle school. I like feeling like I have the power. I
3 don't want to go back to being the low man on the totem
4 pole. I like it up here at the top. Looking down on all the
5 young sixth graders and seeing how scared they are. I
6 remember how that feels and I don't want to do it all over
7 again.

8   Being a freshman is going to be intimidating! How will I
9 know where to go? The school is huge. The seniors are
10 huge. They look like college students. I'm nowhere close to
11 being their size. I'll look like an elementary school student
12 compared to them.

13   Why can't they just add another year on to middle
14 school? That would work perfect. I could stay here, in this
15 school, where I know where everything is and I know all the
16 teachers and they know me. I could stay at the top instead
17 of starting all over again. And then maybe next year I'd be
18 ready. I'd be older. Stronger. Bigger. And I'd be happy to be
19 starting high school and moving on. I would. I wouldn't even
20 complain about it. I swear!

21   We're just too young to be thrown into the wolves like
22 that. Can't they see that they're rushing us? We're not ready
23 to be the little fish in a big, huge pond! I might not even
24 have class with any of my friends. What then? I'll be all
25 alone! No one will sit with me. No one will talk to me. I'll be
26 an outcast. I'll probably end up talking to myself and
27 becoming that weird kid that everyone gossips about.
28 They'll throw spitballs at me and trip me when I walk down

1   the hall. I'll be a walking human target.

2   Tonight I'm going to talk to my parents about holding

3   me back. There's no way they'll want to subject me to

4   torture like that.

39. The Sacrifice

(Girl)

1   I have this thing about my hair. I love it. I love the feel
2   of it. I love the smell of it. I love the color of it. I love the
3   way it curls. I love the way it straightens. I love the way it
4   looks wet. Or dry. Or when it gets windblown. I love how
5   long it is. How it feels when I wear it down and when I wear
6   it up. I really love it when it's braided. French braids.
7   Fishtail braids. English braids. Twist braids. Any kind of
8   braid you can imagine. Tiny braids and thick braids. I love
9   them all!
10   That's why I know what I have to do. It came to me the
11   other day in church when the minister was talking about
12   sacrifice and how for something to be a real sacrifice it has
13   to be something you really love or want. Giving up
14   something you don't really care about isn't a sacrifice at all.
15   Makes sense. It sure hasn't ever hurt me to donate old
16   clothes that I either can't fit into or are out of style anyway.
17   Or to bag up toys that I haven't played with in years. I didn't
18   even mind donating my cell phone last year but that's
19   because I knew I was getting a better one for my birthday.
20   A real sacrifice has to affect you in some way. Has to
21   make you stop and think. Maybe even make you choose
22   between doing something for yourself or doing something for
23   somebody else.
24   That's why I've decided to donate my hair. Twelve whole
25   inches of it. So that they can make wigs for people who have
26   cancer. I hope my hair goes to a little girl and that she loves
27   it as much as I do. I can see her, twirling it between her
28   fingers, smiling at herself in the mirror. I focus on her so

1   that I don't change my mind.

2   I know this really is a sacrifice because it's the hardest

3   thing I've ever done. That's why I also know that it's

4   probably the best thing I've ever done.

40. Why Was I Born?

(Girl or Guy)

1   "Every life has a purpose. What is yours?"
2   That's the essay question we have to answer in English
3   class. I thought it would be easy. I'd just jot something
4   stupid down, like "create a cure for cancer" and I'd be done.
5   Not to say that curing cancer is stupid, but the answer
6   would be so lame. So predictable. Like who wouldn't want
7   to believe that their life would be so important that they
8   would do something amazing like that for the human race?
9   But what if my life is more simple than that? What if I
10 don't do anything that amazing, that great, or that
11 memorable for myself or society? What if I just end up living
12 a day-in-and-day-out kind of life where I leave no stamp in
13 history? Surely I would still have a purpose. A reason for
14 existing.
15 Maybe I would only touch one life. One single person
16 whose life would be altered because of me. Maybe I wouldn't
17 even know it. Maybe I would be driving one day and my car
18 would die and the person behind me would be delayed from
19 getting on the interstate and being involved in a horrible life-
20 changing accident.
21 Maybe I would never know the purpose of my life. I would
22 spend my whole life searching for meaning, never knowing
23 that I wasn't ever supposed to figure it out. I was just
24 supposed to "be" and that would be enough. Would that
25 make me a failure? Not knowing why I was put on this
26 earth?
27 But what if that's the real answer. That you only find out
28 your purpose *after* you're dead and gone? Wouldn't that be

1   great? To see a slideshow of your life and see how you *did*
2   affect history and didn't even know it? That all the
3   meaningless things in life really did have meaning? So I
4   guess the answer to the question of "What is my purpose?"
5   is *everything*. I just don't get to know it all yet.

41. Night and Day

(Guy)

1   My brother and I are like night and day. He's a slob and
2 I'm not. He eats like a pig and I eat like a bird. He loves
3 sports and I love computers. He has had about fifteen
4 girlfriends — just this year — and I've never had one. He
5 loves chips and cookies and I love carrots and hummus. We
6 are complete opposites of each other. I swear one of us is
7 adopted and if you look at my parents, I tend to think that
8 it's probably me.

9   Certainly my dad didn't marry my mom for her
10 housekeeping or cooking skills and yet he can plate up at
11 least three times at dinner, just like my brother. Between
12 the two of them I don't know how we afford groceries.
13 Probably why my mom always buys the cheap, unhealthy
14 stuff. Forget fresh vegetables and fruit — way too expensive.
15 Doesn't matter what I want. I'm outnumbered three to one.

16   What's worse is that they expect me to live with my
17 brother. In the same room! His side looks like a war zone
18 and my side looks like a hospital room. Neat and clean. Or
19 what I like to think of as "livable." I won't even step foot on
20 his side. It's disgusting. No telling what kind of germs are
21 hibernating over there. He has dishes with food still on them
22 and glasses half-filled with soda that have mold growing on
23 top. But knowing him, that won't even stop him from
24 drinking it one night when he's too lazy to get up and get a
25 new one.

26   The smell is killing me. He's got sweaty workout clothes
27 all over his floor and his sneakers could knock an elephant
28 over. I go through three cans of air freshener a week. I have

1 even thought about wearing a mask. But even that wouldn't
2 help. This funk can penetrate anything! I can't wait until the
3 day I move out. I will have to think long and hard about
4 whether I will even let any of them visit. I have to be adopted
5 because this cannot be my real family.

42. Ban on Soda

(Girl or Guy)

1   There are worse things in life than soda. Would somebody
2 *please* tell my mother that? Everyone should be allowed one
3 little vice, right? Mine is soda. It's not like I drink a twelve
4 pack every day and it's not like I couldn't quit drinking it if I
5 wanted to. I just choose not to. I like the taste of it. I like
6 the bubbles. I like the caffeine. What's the harm in that?
7 Millions of people in the world drink soda. Why can't I?
8   She's such a hypocrite, too. Telling me how bad it is for
9 me. What about the stuff she eats? She thinks nothing of
10 having at least four chocolate cookies as a before-bedtime
11 snack. Every night. What about all the sugar in those
12 things? Not to mention the artificial stuff. They're full of
13 preservatives and chemicals, too. So why can she eat those
14 but I can't drink my sodas?
15   Know what she wants me to drink instead? Fruit juice.
16 Or smoothies. Well, guess what, Mom? They're full of sugar,
17 too. She even had the nerve to tell me that I could drink
18 water instead. Just plain old out-of-the-tap water. Not even
19 bottled. Not even flavored. Just water. No fizz. No sugar.
20 Nothing. What's the point of that? I might as well drink *air!*
21   Well, I'll show her. I'll take up a different bad habit. I'll
22 switch from pretzels to chips! Good old greasy, fat-laden
23 chips. Not the baked or light kind either. Full-blown chips!
24 And I'll eat them a bag at a time. I'm not playin'! And
25 maybe I'll start eating ice cream. Every night. On top of a
26 brownie. With whipped cream. And a cherry. You'll see,
27 Mom. You'll wish all I ever did was drink soda!

43. Now That's Exciting

(Girl or Guy)

1   So I waited all year for that? Three hundred sixty-five
2 days to hit my next birthday to get a gift card? Are you
3 being serious? I'm a teenager now. Not a pre-teen. Isn't that
4 some sort of milestone or something? Don't I deserve more
5 than a Walmart gift card? What do I even need or want from
6 there? Oh sure, there's lots to buy there. But come on! As
7 a birthday gift? Yeah, I want to buy my own underwear, or
8 shampoo, or deodorant. They might as well have bought me
9 a McDonald's gift card so I can buy my own food, too.
10   I guess I was naïve to think I might even get a surprise
11 party or something. I mean I am a teenager now. It's not like
12 I expected pony rides and big blow up bouncy toys on the
13 front lawn, but I did expect something. How can they treat
14 this like any other birthday? Or even worse than any other
15 birthday. Surely they don't think I've outgrown parties and
16 stuff? Just because I'm thirteen? Come on. I'm not *that* old.
17 I'm still just a kid. Barely out of elementary school. I'm not
18 too old for cake and ice cream and balloons. Well ... I could
19 live without the balloons. But who doesn't want cake on
20 their birthday? Now I don't even get to make a wish! What
21 kind of lame birthday doesn't even include a birthday wish?
22   This is the worst birthday ever. Even worse than that
23 year when I had the chicken pox and none of my friends
24 were allowed to come over. Or the year that I got a coat as
25 a birthday present. I'd say it's even worse than the year my
26 dog got hit by a car. You know, come to think of it, I never
27 *do* have good birthdays. Why should this year be any
28 different? Just because I'm thirteen? Think about it.

1   Thirteen is the most unlucky number around. I was destined
2   to have a horrible day.
3   Well, at least I've got Christmas to look forward to.

44. People Watching

(Girl)

1   Do you ever people watch? Just hang out somewhere
2   and watch the people go by? I do! In fact, I'm kind of
3   addicted to it. There are so many weirdos it's hard to stop.
4   My favorite place is the mall. Luckily I live close enough to
5   walk to it. I go there almost every day after school. My
6   friends think I'm a shopaholic, but I never even buy
7   anything. I just love hanging out there.

8   Some people are freaks, let me tell you. I saw a guy and
9   a girl hooked together by a chain. I'm for real. Like either he
10 or she was a dog or something. I guess they were afraid of
11 losing each other? *(Laugh)*

12 Just like some parents I see with their kids on a leash.
13 I know it's supposed to be for their safety, but holy cow!
14 How can that even feel right? Tugging on your kid like it's a
15 rambunctious puppy. What's next? Obedience school where
16 they learn to heel?

17 I love the hair, too. All the colors of the rainbow.
18 Whenever I see someone with neon hair I try to figure out
19 where they work. 'Cause who would hire someone like that?
20 I can't really picture them being a teacher or a doctor or
21 anything. Especially the ones with the multi-colored hair. If
22 a teacher of mine walked in looking like that, I wouldn't be
23 able to concentrate on what they were saying.

24 The best is the clothes. It was freezing out the other day
25 — I'm talking below zero — and I totally saw a guy wearing
26 shorts. *Shorts!* Like it's the middle of summer or something.
27 And to beat it all, he had on flip-flops, too. Now you see why
28 I'm addicted? It's like a totally crazy world out here.

45. Invited/Uninvited

(Girl)

1   My best friend totally rocks. Well, she did. See, she
2   invited me to her friend's sixteen birthday bash where all the
3   guests get to ride in a limo and get a hundred dollar gift card
4   for a shopping spree at the mall *and* go to this really ritzy
5   place for dinner. Afterward, a movie with popcorn, candy,
6   and a soda. And all of it was paid for. Completely free. And
7   completely unbelievable!

8   At my house we are never allowed to get popcorn at the
9   movies. And if we want something to drink, we have to
10 smuggle a water bottle in our jacket or something. Mom
11 says the cost of the movie is too much to add on snacks.
12 So I was really looking forward to having some serious
13 munchies while watching the movie. I didn't even care that
14 it was a stupid horror film. Figured I'd be too busy eating to
15 pay much attention anyway.

16 So of course I'm disappointed that I don't get to go
17 anymore. Like, for real, a hundred dollar gift card? For
18 nothing? I don't even get that much on my birthday or at
19 Christmas. I had already gone online and figured out what I
20 was going to buy at each store. It completely stinks that my
21 friend has "uninvited" me. I didn't even think you could do
22 that! No take-backs, you know?

23 And it's all because of her stupid new boyfriend. Her
24 first, I might add. Clearly she's going to be one of those
25 friends who completely ditches her friends whenever she
26 has a boyfriend. She's been with him a week and he gets
27 top priority over me? I've been her friend for years and this
28 is how she treats me. I don't even want to see her face right

1   now. I'm not going to be her sloppy seconds.

2   *(Pause and look to side)* **Really? Thomas can't go now?**

3   **Yeah, I'm still open. Cool! See you later.**

4   *(Look to audience)* **Oh come on. Don't look at me that**

5   **way. I'm not completely stupid. It's the mall. And popcorn!**

6   **And candy!** *(Rush off)*

46. Torn Between Friends

(Girl)

1 My friends have started this whole "Hatfields and
2 McCoys" thing between our two sets of friends. On one
3 hand I have my band friends and on the other I have my
4 track friends. It's always been totally cool that way. No one
5 seemed to care. But then Jenni got in a fight with Kara and
6 now all of a sudden it's absolutely forbidden for all of us to
7 be friends. It's so stupid. I feel like we should carry around
8 pitchforks and blacken our teeth or something like the
9 original hillbillies. Thank goodness I don't have a boyfriend
10 on "the other side" or it'd be like *Romeo and Juliet*.

11   So how am I supposed to choose between these two
12 sets of friends? I love them both. My band friends are goofy
13 and fun and love to just hang out and listen to music.
14 Sometimes we have jam sessions and on really goofy nights
15 we sing karaoke. Why would I want to give that up? But then
16 my track friends are fun, too. We like to stay up all night and
17 watch scary movies and then do these ridiculous runs as the
18 sun comes up. Sounds lame, I know, but if you were a
19 runner, you'd get it.

20   I don't want to have to cross enemy lines just to be with
21 one or the other. Why can't they see how crazy this all is?
22 Two people get in a fight and we *all* have to suffer? Why are
23 we giving Jenni and Kara that much power? We don't need
24 them telling us who we can be friends with, do we? I think
25 it's time for a good old revolution. Maybe if I make the first
26 move, the rest will follow. I'll be like a diplomat bringing
27 peace to both sides.

28   But what if they both hate me? I'll be all alone. Like the

1   man without a country. No one will speak to me. I'll have to
2   sit alone at lunch and won't ever leave my house. It's no use
3   ... I just have to choose ... but how? *(Pull out a quarter)* **OK.**
4   Here goes. Heads for Hatfields.

47. Beauty School Bound

(Girl)

1   I love doing hair. I get up two hours early every day just
2 so I have time to really do my hair right for school. No
3 ponytails or braids for this girl. No way. I'm talking prom
4 hair every day. With lots of curls and a million bobby pins.
5 My friends tease me about it. Like why would anyone wear
6 that kind of hair with a pair of jeans and a sweatshirt? But
7 I don't care. In fact, I say "why not"? Why not have fabulous
8 hair with jeans and a sweatshirt? Just because you dress
9 down for a day, doesn't mean your hair should dress down,
10 too. Besides, who notices what you wear when you have an
11 awesome hairdo?

12   I love doing my friends' hair, too. Sometimes I think it's
13 the only reason they invite me over. Just so I'll play around
14 with their hair. But I really don't mind because it gives me
15 practice. If I'm lucky, they even let me cut it. I guess you
16 could say that hair is my life.

17   That's why I don't understand what the big deal is. Why
18 do I have to go to college when I'd rather go to beauty
19 school? My parents are completely freaking out about it. For
20 no reason. Who says beauty school isn't just as great as
21 college? It's just as expensive! So that should prove
22 something to them. They think that just because high
23 school is coming up that I have to be on the fast track to
24 some Ivy League college. Right now. Well, I don't even want
25 to go to college. Much less some fancy Ivy League one. I
26 want to do hair.

27   It's completely respectable and I can make a good living
28 at it. Maybe I'll even do hair for the stars. Move to California

1   and be a famous hairstylist of the rich and famous. Instead
2   of forcing me into college, they should be moving me out
3   west to the land of opportunity. Don't waste money on
4   college, set me up in an apartment in Hollywood. Look at
5   this hair — who wouldn't be knocking on my door?

48. Addicted to the Beach

(Girl)

1   I think that in a past life I must've been a mermaid or
2 something. I cannot drag myself out of the water. It is so
3 calm and peaceful and like a whole other world under there.
4 Completely quiet and full of new things every day. How can
5 my parents possibly move to Kentucky? Don't they see how
6 landlocked that state is? There isn't an ocean close for
7 days. How can I live in a place like that? I'll be like a fish
8 out of water. Yeah, it's corny, I know. But it's true. I can't
9 live without the ocean. Haven't they always told me that I
10 swim like a fish and that I could've been raised by dolphins?
11 Can't they see how cruel it is to make me move to a place
12 like that?
13   How will I even sleep? The sound of the ocean has been
14 in my ears all my life. The sound of the waves crashing has
15 put me to sleep since I was a baby. You can't rip a person
16 from that. I'll become an insomniac. A walking zombie. I'll
17 have bags under my eyes and be so tired I won't be able to
18 function in school. Is that what they want for their daughter?
19   And what about the sand? The warm sand that squishes
20 between your toes? It warms you up from the soles of your
21 feet to the top of your head. You can't replace that with cold,
22 hard dirt. My feet will become calloused. Insensitive.
23 Unfeeling. It won't matter if I walk on the ground or tarmac.
24 I won't even be able to tell. It's like losing a seventh sense
25 or something.
26   My mom says I should be grateful. That some people
27 never ever get to visit a beach much less live on one for
28 twelve years. Well, how can I be grateful for that? They don't

1   know what they're missing. I *do!* It's like torture to take it

2   away from me now. I don't believe that stupid quote, "It's

3   better to have loved and lost than never to have loved at

4   all." I love it all so much. Please don't make me leave it.

5   *Please!*

49. The Itsy-Bitsy Crazy Mother

(Girl or Guy)

1   I don't see why my mother's irrational fear of spiders
2   gets to dictate what kind of pet I can have. It's completely
3   unfair. Just because she thinks spiders are creepy and
4   crawly and "icky," as she puts it, doesn't mean I think that
5   way. Spiders are cool! And she is way out of control. I'm
6   serious. One day I came home from school to find her up on
7   a chair, holding a broom like it was a shotgun or something,
8   and seriously freaking out because there was an itsy-bitsy
9   spider that had run underneath the couch. She wouldn't
10 even get off the chair!
11   Another time she woke the whole house up by
12 screaming bloody murder because she found a spider in the
13 shower. That was fun. Being woken up out of a dead sleep
14 to see my mother running naked around the house like a
15 crazy person. Does she not ever realize how irrational it all
16 is? She's like a thousand times bigger than the thing.
17 They're just harmless little creatures trying to live out their
18 lives in peace. I'm one hundred percent sure that they are
19 more afraid of the crazy woman than she is of them.
20   So why should her neurotic behavior impact *my* life?
21 This is the chance of a lifetime to own a real live tarantula.
22 I wouldn't even have to pay a dime for it because my friend's
23 mother is making him give it away. You guessed it. Another
24 neurotic mother. But this could totally work. A free pet that
25 doesn't take up much space and doesn't cost a lot to feed
26 and my mom says no? Without even really thinking about it?

1 Tara, that's the tarantula, is completely harmless. Even if
2 she did bite you, it's nothing worse than a bee sting. Well,
3 not unless you're allergic to them ... but that's beside the
4 point. I'm sure no one in this house is allergic. Does my
5 mom have any idea how cool it would be to tell my friends
6 that I own a tarantula?
7   Come on, Mom! I promise it will hardly ever get out of the
8 cage. And when it does, I won't even make you look for it.

50. My Mother Is a Witch

(Girl)

1   My mother is a witch. Like for real. Not in the mean, she-
2   makes-me-do-chores kind of way, but in the waving-a-wand-
3   and-doing-spells kind of way. I'm serious. She has spell
4   books and potions and weird figurines all over our house.
5   And she hides this freaky looking wand thing under her
6   pillow every night as if she's afraid she's going to be
7   attacked. By who? Who knows. I'm not really sure who
8   attacks witches. Warlocks? Dragons? You tell me. It's her
9   crazy world. Not mine.
10   She even has this group of friends that she calls her
11   "coven." They come over at least once a week and burn
12   incense and talk in a mumbo jumbo crazy kind of way. They
13   think they cast spells and stuff against the people who are
14   out to get them. Like their bosses. Or mother-in-laws. Or
15   the butcher at the grocery store who charges them too
16   much for their meat. It is bizarre to say the least.
17   I'm OK with letting my mom think she's a witch. Black
18   cauldron and all. Especially since she's good enough to keep
19   all this at home. But now she thinks I'm coming of age into
20   witchcraft. That this is the year I will blossom into a full-
21   fledged witch like her. How can I possibly go along with
22   that? I don't want to be a witch, real or imagined! I wouldn't
23   even know how to act or what to say. But when I tell her
24   that, she says that I have to complete the training. Like a
25   witch boot camp of sorts. She even says I can skip school
26   to do it. Now, that's tempting for sure, but who knows what
27   these crazy people will do to me? They might carve
28   something into my skin, or make me drink something with

1   a frog's head poking out of it.

2   I didn't want to do this, but I think it's time I called my

3   dad. It's high time he knew just what kind of crazy world

4   he's left me to live in. I just hope and pray that he doesn't

5   think he's a warlock!

51. How Can I Miss You When You Don't Ever Leave?

(Girl)

1 My boyfriend is super clingy. Like moss on a tree. Or
2 melted cheese on a pizza. He thinks we should be
3 inseparable. Not to say that he's all over me or anything. In
4 fact, we've never even held hands. He's clingy in a
5 completely emotional way. Ever since I said yes that I would
6 go out with him, he thinks he owns me. Every second of my
7 life.

8 In between classes. Bam. He's there. Waiting outside
9 the door of my class. I don't even know how he gets there
10 so fast. I think maybe he gets the teacher to let him out
11 early or something. After school on the way to the bus. He's
12 there. When I get home and get online, he's there.
13 Messaging me immediately. Later, it's a never-ending phone
14 call. He's completely suffocating me!

15 If we go five seconds without communicating, he texts
16 me things like "I miss you." Then, he'll ask, "Do you miss
17 me?" How can I miss the guy? He doesn't ever leave! You
18 have to go without something to actually miss it. I don't
19 know why he can't see that. Hasn't he ever heard that
20 "Absence makes the heart grow fonder"? He doesn't even
21 give me a chance to miss him.

22 But how do you tell someone that you are quickly getting
23 to the point that just the sight of him makes you gag? It's
24 like gorging on your favorite food. You might love it at first,
25 like a never-ending bowl of mint chocolate chip ice cream,
26 but pretty soon you'd put down the spoon and hope that you

1 never ever see it again. That's how I feel about Jerry. I just
2 want some space. I need time to digest all this sugary
3 sweetness. If he doesn't back off soon, I'm going to change
4 my phone number. Maybe I'll even be homeschooled. Come
5 on, Jer-bear, enough is enough.

52. A Little Overboard

(Girl)

1   My new boyfriend is a little out of control. For Valentine's
2   Day, he bought me a stuffed teddy bear, a single red rose,
3   *and* a bracelet with my birthstone. Don't get me wrong.
4   These are all very sweet things for a girl to get, and I
5   thought I would like being the pampered girlfriend. It always
6   made me jealous to see other girls getting treated that way.
7   But I was wrong.

8   Do you know what kind of pressure that brings? What's
9   next? A diamond ring? How can I ever compete with gifts
10   like that? I thought writing him a really sweet note would be
11   good enough. I never dreamed I had to buy him an actual
12   gift! We're only thirteen years old.

13   My parents aren't like his. They won't fund me buying
14   gifts for a guy in middle school. And I don't want to spend
15   all my saved-up birthday money on gifts for a boyfriend. I
16   don't mean to sound selfish, but come on. That money was
17   given to me to spend on me! I already have a list of things
18   I want to buy.

19   And now *his* birthday is coming up. What am I supposed
20   to get him? I already feel bad that I didn't get him a
21   Valentine's gift after all he did for me. I'll be the worst
22   girlfriend in the world if I don't do something really special.

23   That's why I only have one choice. I have to break up
24   with him *before* his birthday. *Before* he figures out that I only
25   got him a lame birthday card that plays music and a picture
26   I drew of his dog. Even though I did a really good job on it.
27   But a stupid picture can't compare to stuffed bears and
28   roses and jewelry! He'll think I'm cheap. Well, guess what?

1   I am! But this isn't my fault. It's his. He totally ruined things
2   by going overboard. After all, it was Valentine's Day. Not
3   Christmas!

53. All Made Up

(Girl)

1   My mother is driving me crazy. She thinks that just
2 because she was a model starting at a young age that I
3 should be, too. She won't let up on me. Every time I walk
4 out of the house, she wants me to be picture perfect. Perfect
5 outfit. Perfect shoes. Perfect hair. Perfect makeup. In fact, it
6 doesn't even matter if I leave the house. She wants me that
7 way all the time. My mother is the kind of woman who puts
8 on her full face of makeup even if she knows she's staying
9 home all day. I don't think I've ever seen her without
10 makeup or in a pair of sweats. The woman never stops
11 looking like she's ready for a photo shoot.
12   But that's not me. I hate hair and makeup and tight-
13 fitting clothes. I absolutely *love* wearing sweatpants. They're
14 so comfortable! Not that I ever do at home. I have to wear
15 them at my friend's house when I sleep over there.
16   The shoes are the worst. High heels for everything. Even
17 jeans. My feet are always killing me. When I complain, she
18 always says things about "there's a price for beauty,
19 honey." Well, I don't want to pay that price. I'm OK not
20 being beautiful. I'm OK being average. I'm OK *not* being a
21 model. Why won't she listen to me? I am not a doll that she
22 can dress up. She might have gotten away with that when I
23 was little — you should see the pictures she took of me as
24 a baby! I think she drug me to every baby beauty pageant
25 in the state. I never even placed in one.
26   You'd think she'd get a clue. I am not a model like she
27 was. I am a normal, average girl who doesn't want to put on
28 three layers of mascara just to go to the library. Do you

1 think I can call Social Services? Surely forcing your
2 daughter into makeup, heels, and prom hair is some kind of
3 abuse?

54. An Unsung Hero

(Guy)

1   Dear Mr. Gibson,

2   I am writing this letter to you to tell you some things
3 that I can never tell you to your face. Well, I could, but you
4 had to go and move away to another school. Budget cuts
5 stink. You were the best teacher this school ever had. It
6 shouldn't have been you.

7   I wanted you to know that you are the reason I stopped
8 getting in trouble at school. I haven't had detention this
9 whole year. Believe me, that's a record. I owe it all to you.
10 I'll never forget that day when you saw me pound a hole in
11 the wall in the locker room. You could've turned me in.
12 Gotten me into a lot of trouble. But you didn't. You made
13 me stay after class so you could find out why. You didn't yell
14 or embarrass me in front of everyone. And then you made
15 me come after school every day and you helped me fix it.
16 And while we did, you talked to me. Like you really cared
17 about my parents getting divorced and my dad moving
18 away. You didn't jump to conclusions that day. Didn't label
19 me a punk like most teachers did. You saw that I was
20 hurting and you helped me a lot.

21   I'll never forget you telling me to "man up" for my mom.
22 I wanted you to know that I'm trying. I don't want to hurt
23 her anymore. I know that she's gone through a lot. Like me.
24 I think she's surprised that I'm actually helping out around
25 the house and not hanging out with my friends as much as
26 I used to.

27   You're a great teacher, Mr. Gibson. I'm sure you don't
28 hear that a lot. Kids my age are too busy bucking against

1   authority to ever stop and say thank you. Just know that
2   what you do doesn't go unnoticed even though you might
3   not ever hear it. You made a real difference in my life.
4   Thanks for believing in me, even when I didn't.
5   Always your student and friend,
6   Tyler

55. Unwanted Pizza

(Girl or Guy)

1   Geez. Can you say "overreact"? It's not like we pulled
2 the fire alarm or anything. Mrs. Hill is going ballistic over
3 nothing. Where's her sense of humor? It was pretty funny
4 seeing the pizza guy show up at her door in the middle of
5 class. Her face was priceless. Especially when he held out
6 ten boxes of pizzas!

7   She could barely get the words out, "I did *not* order any
8 pizzas." She wasn't happy at all when he pulled out the bill
9 and repeated her phone number back to her.

10   "Well, clearly someone hijacked my phone while I was in
11 the hall," she told the delivery guy. But he didn't really care.
12 He just wanted his money. Fifty-two dollars and thirty-nine
13 cents. Not bad for ten pizzas. At least we made sure we got
14 the buy-one, get-one-free special. You'd think she could've
15 been happy about that! But she was *far* from happy. I can
16 still hear the door slamming and the look on her flushed
17 face when she turned back around to the class.

18   "I'll give ten pizzas to the first person who tells me who
19 is responsible for this," she said. I have to admit, that was
20 pretty smart of her. I almost thought someone would crack
21 and rat us out. But no one did.

22   "Fine then. Detention every day after school for two
23 weeks, and *I'll* eat the pizza." She opened the top box and
24 ate at least three slices of pizza while she sat and glared at
25 all of us.

26   Two weeks of detention and *she* gets the pizzas? How's
27 that fair?

56. Negative Nelly

(Guy)

1   I have this friend Nelson who we've renamed Negative
2 Nelly. He drives us all crazy. He can never see the good in
3 anything. He's like the world's worst Eeyore. Gloom and
4 doom about everything. You think I'm exaggerating but I'm
5 not.

6   His parents took him to the Bahamas last year and you
7 know what he said? Too hot. The year before — Rome. Too
8 dirty. The year before that was Myrtle Beach. Too
9 commercialized.

10   Everything is too much. Too crowded. Too predictable.
11 Too dramatic. Too soft. Too loud. Too spicy. Too bland. Too
12 scary. Too boring. Nothing is ever "just right." I mean
13 nothing. How can you find anything wrong with Rome or the
14 Bahamas? Does he even understand how lucky he is to go
15 to these places? I've never even left Maine in my life. Not
16 that Maine's not great, but come on! Rome? Who complains
17 about going to Rome?

18   I truly believe that if Negative Nelly dies and goes to
19 heaven, he'll find something to complain about. It's *too*
20 bright. Or *too* angelic. Or *too* crowded. Well ... let's hope on
21 that last part, right?

22   But seriously, I don't think anything will ever make this
23 guy happy. He's destined to be alone the rest of his life.
24 Don't even try to get him a girlfriend. Too tall. Too short. Too
25 chatty. Too quiet. Too smart. Too dumb. I would love to
26 personally remove the word *too* from his vocabulary.

27   You know what, Nelson, you are *too* much!

57. That Is Not an Angel

(Girl)

1   Why can't my mom stand up for *our* traditions? I know
2 that when you combine two families that you have to make
3 compromises, but I feel like his side is getting everything.
4 Who wants to open presents on Christmas day? We've
5 always done ours on Christmas Eve. After we all go to
6 church. It might as well be Christmas day because it's so
7 late. So why would we want to try and sleep and then get
8 up early in the morning? It doesn't even make sense.
9   And then there's the angel for the tree. We've been using
10 the same one my whole life. Sure she's gotten a little ratty
11 looking, but she's still awesome. And that's what's
12 supposed to go on a tree. An angel or a star. Whoever heard
13 of a shiny Roman-looking thing as a topper? It's not even a
14 star. In fact, I don't know what it's supposed to be! It looks
15 like our tree is going into battle or something. I don't care if
16 it's been in his family for seventy-five years. So has my
17 grandma and we don't stick her up there!
18   Well, if this is Christmas, I hate to see what our Easter
19 is going to be like. Will we totally nix our pie eating contest
20 and outdoor egg hunt? And what about the prize tickets?
21 Will those go away too? Will we be reduced to hiding real
22 hardboiled eggs and not getting candy in our baskets? Will
23 Mom and I have to wear matching Easter bonnets and pose
24 for a hideous family photo?
25   I want to keep our traditions alive. I want to save our
26 angel. Maybe we should have two trees. And *two*
27 Christmases. That's the answer. One on Christmas Eve and
28 one on Christmas. What's the harm in that? Now, that's real
29 compromise if you ask me. This way everyone is happy.

58. The Naked Dream

(Girl or Guy)

1   I think I need to see the counselor. Or maybe some sort
2   of professional therapist who specializes in dreams. It can't
3   be normal to keep having the same dream night after night.
4   It doesn't matter what I do before bed: what I eat or drink,
5   what time I go to bed, what I watch on television. It's always
6   the same dream. I don't even want to go to sleep anymore
7   because I know that any time I close my eyes, I'm going to
8   see myself standing naked in the school hallway. Or the
9   school gymnasium. Or the school cafeteria. Or on the
10 school bus. Always somewhere at school. Completely buck
11 naked.
12   I'm always running. Trying to find a way to hide my
13 naked body. And everyone is always pointing and laughing
14 and making fun of me. Well, to be fair, why wouldn't they
15 be? Who would ever go to school naked? It's completely
16 humiliating! And even though I try to tell myself that it's a
17 dream, even while I'm dreaming, it never feels like it is. The
18 panic I feel is real. Not imagined. Every time I wake up, my
19 heart is pounding like crazy. I'm practically hyperventilating.
20   There has to be a reason why I keep dreaming about
21 this. Maybe it's from way back when I had naked baby
22 pictures. In the tub. With some well-placed bubbles. It
23 could've scarred me. Or that year when my bathing suit
24 came down after I jumped off the diving board. Even though
25 my parents swore that no one saw me. That really could've
26 scarred me. Or maybe it's because my mom made me dress
27 up as the Grinch one year in school and made me wear
28 tights. I sure felt naked. That *definitely* scarred me. Clearly

1   all these near-naked events have warped my mind.
2   This can't be normal. Please, somebody stop my naked
3   dreams!

59. The Perfect Person

(Girl)

1   Do you ever wish that you could design yourself? Come
2 up with the perfect DNA strand to make yourself the perfect
3 person? What would you put on your checklist of traits that
4 you just had to have?
5   I would definitely want a fabulous singing voice instead
6 of the off-key screecher I've got now. And I'd be really smart
7 so that I could write songs that would change the world. As
8 far as looks go, I'd have super white straight teeth. The kind
9 that almost look fake because they're so perfect. And my
10 hair would be shiny and straight and not frizzy in the least
11 little bit.
12   My skin would not have a blemish on it. Perfectly pale
13 with no moles or freckles. Almost like a porcelain doll.
14 People would say that I had "photogenic looks" because I
15 would never take a bad picture, not even if I was making
16 silly faces or caught off guard. I would be tall and have the
17 perfect body. Muscles in all the right places. Strong, healthy
18 bones that would help me be athletic and fit. And my
19 coordination would be perfect, too. No more clumsy falls or
20 awkward strolls through the hallways. I would be graceful
21 like a gazelle and practically float through school. I wouldn't
22 trip down or up the stairs and would never ever fall flat on
23 my face in the middle of an assembly.
24   Because of being so perfect, I would be rich. The richest
25 person in town. Only I wouldn't be greedy, I would be
26 generous. Charitable and loving. No one would go hungry if
27 I was around. So my DNA would have to contain a strain of
28 humility so that I wouldn't take it all for granted. I wouldn't

1   forget what it's like to *not* be perfect.

2   That's my checklist. What's yours?

60. The Thought Doesn't Always Count

(Guy)

1   My grandma is the pits at Christmas shopping. Her gifts
2 are the absolute worst you can imagine. I'm talking far
3 beyond the horrible snowman sweater or handmade knitted
4 mittens. It's like she goes to the store thinking, "What
5 would my grandson want for Christmas?" so that she can
6 buy the complete opposite of that. I think she's totally
7 bought into that bull about it "being the thought that
8 counts."
9   Well maybe that would be true if she actually did put
10 some thought into it. Seriously, how hard can it be? I'm a
11 teenage boy. Go to the electronics department. There really
12 isn't anything there I wouldn't love to have. I'd even settle
13 for the automotive department. Buy me something for the
14 car I will one day own. So what if I can't use it for a few
15 years. At least I *will* use it eventually. Last resort, go to the
16 music department. Don't buy me any bands that you
17 recognize the name of, and it will work out great. No more
18 "Best of Elvis" or "World's Greatest Frank Sinatra Hits."
19 OK, Grandma? Buy me something that I want. Or will use.
20   Unlike the nail clipper combo face trimmer set she
21 bought me last year. The nail clippers had jewels on them.
22 And look at this face — do I look like I need a beard
23 trimmer? The year before I got socks. Lots and lots of
24 socks. Which might have actually been an improvement on
25 prior years except they were colored socks. With patterns
26 and stripes and characters from children's shows. One pair

1   even had little elves on them. Did she really think I would be
2   caught dead in any of those?
3   Mom said that this year Grandma is giving gift cards,
4   which I'm totally psyched about. I might actually get
5   something I can use this year ... except ... oh no! I bet I get
6   a card to her favorite store: The Copper Candle! What am I
7   going to do with that?

61. The Wheelbarrow Ride

(Girl or Guy)

1 My parents are bizarre. Always have been, always will
2 be. I think it's because they were born in the Sixties or
3 something. Because of them, my brothers and sister and I
4 have endured the strangest traditions. When I was young, I
5 thought all families did things like ours. It didn't take long
6 to realize how very wrong I was. The worst, and most public,
7 were the wheelbarrow rides.

8 See, my parents are runners. At least they were when
9 the tradition first started. In a go-green kind of way, they
10 decided that the first day of school would always
11 incorporate a run to school — with us in the kid carrier. You
12 know. The kind that runners run behind. But soon we
13 outgrew the runner's cart. And, to be honest, they became
14 less enthused runners.

15 Not about to let the tradition die, they decided it would
16 be great to put us in a yellow wheelbarrow — you know,
17 yellow like a school bus — for our first day of school. I have
18 to admit that we even thought it was pretty cool, at first. No
19 other kids arrived to school in a wheelbarrow. But as we got
20 older, we started feeling a little ridiculous. Come on, we
21 were in a wheelbarrow.

22 But my parents were adamant about keeping up the
23 tradition. When we hit middle school and wouldn't easily
24 comply, they bribed us. If we rode to school every year in
25 the wheelbarrow all the way through high school — yes, you
26 heard that right, *high school* — they would give us one
27 thousand dollars on the first day of our senior year. One
28 thousand dollars! Now, I don't know about you, but that's

1   some serious cash to me. I've planned how to spend that
2   ever since sixth grade. It's like my "If I won the lottery" list.
3   So guess what? Next week when I start high school, I
4   will be arriving in a yellow wheelbarrow. Laugh all you want.
5   And you know what else, when I have kids, I think I'll carry
6   on the tradition.

62. The Gurgling Within

(Guy)

1   Something is definitely wrong with me. It doesn't matter
2 what I eat or what I do, my stomach gurgles like a volcano
3 about to blow. And even though all that commotion is
4 happening on the inside, it sounds like it's coming from the
5 outside. So people around me are always thinking that I'm,
6 you know, passing gas. Which I'm not!
7   The noises are completely ridiculous. Some long. Some
8 short. Some quiet. Some loud. All of them horribly
9 embarrassing. I can't go anywhere quiet because all it takes
10 is one long gurgle and everyone's looking at me. Of course
11 being a student, it's impossible to avoid quiet places. I've
12 even made sure that my grades are the absolute worst so
13 that I can be in the bad kids' classes because they are
14 always louder and rowdier than the smart kids' ones. But
15 even those classes have the occasional quiet moment. And
16 it never fails that my stomach, or intestines, or monster
17 inside of me, decides to rear its ugly head the moment there
18 is a second of silence.
19   Forget the library. I haven't been there in years. It's
20 pretty bad when you get looks for your stomach making too
21 much noise. Like I can help it, people!
22   I always try to pass it off by saying things like, "Man, am
23 I starving!" But come on, they might be the bad kids, but
24 they aren't *that* stupid. No one is starving as much as I
25 would have to be. And it's hard to believe that anyway since
26 you certainly wouldn't look at me and think, "Wow. That
27 kid's starving. Somebody get him something to eat. Fast."
28   So what do I do? It doesn't matter what I feed the

1   gurgling beast — it's out to get me. Humiliate me for the
2   rest of my life. What does it want from me? I'm starting to
3   think that maybe I need an exorcist or something.

63. Biggest Fan

(Guy)

1   My brother and I are super competitive. It's easy to see
2 that we get it honestly. My parents both hate to lose at
3 anything. My mom is often the worst. Truth is, if we play
4 cards with her and she doesn't win, we end up playing half
5 the night until she does get a win because she just can't go
6 to sleep without winning. But I wouldn't really call either of
7 them sore losers because even though they might actually
8 be happy for the person that won, they personally just don't
9 accept defeat. Which, when you think about it, is something
10 to be admired and not condemned. I guess you could say
11 that it's always made my brother and I try harder.

12   We don't take anything for granted. We're not like those
13 kids who just naturally excel without ever really trying. We
14 practice a lot. At everything that's important to us. Band,
15 sports, grades. All of it. Doing poorly just isn't an option.

16   That's why my brother and I were completely prepared
17 for the school basketball tryouts. We'd been practicing after
18 school for months, knowing that the season was about to
19 start. It never even crossed our minds that we both wouldn't
20 make it. Not only because we were so committed, but
21 because we're twins. Identical ones, which means we're
22 basically carbon copies of each other. Clearly if one made
23 the team, so would the other.

24   Apparently, the coach didn't quite see it that way.
25 Somehow one of us succeeded in obtaining a spot on the
26 team. The other did not. And even more surprisingly, I was
27 the lucky one. Do you have any idea how awful it is to walk
28 away from a roster and not see your brother's name on it?

1   I couldn't even be excited about making the team! Didn't
2   *want* to be excited about it. I was ready to quit before I even
3   started — and quitting is definitely not something allowed in
4   my house.
5   I figured my brother would be crushed and rightfully so.
6   But as I said before, doing poorly just isn't an option in my
7   family. Not even when it comes to losing. Even though I
8   knew he had to be disappointed, my brother never ever
9   showed it. He was the first to congratulate me and never
10 missed one of my games. I only hope that if the opposite
11 had happened that I would've been so good about it. And
12 even though he didn't make the team, I will always be my
13 brother's biggest fan.

64. Just for Mom

(Girl)

1   I wasn't really the kind of girl who was a fan of tattoos
2 and piercings. To be honest, I just didn't get them or why
3 everyone seemed to want one. Marking up your body
4 permanently just never seemed like a good idea.

5   And then my mom got breast cancer. A lump about the
6 size of a quarter that turned out to be malignant. It was like
7 getting punched in the stomach. For all of us. Even though
8 my mom tried not to show it, I knew she was scared. Really,
9 really scared. Who wouldn't be?

10   My family being like it is, tried to make jokes about it.
11 "Don't be a girl," we'd tell her. "A quarter? That's it? You
12 couldn't even make a half dollar?" That may sound weird to
13 families who handle things differently, but we have always
14 been a family that laughs together. No matter what.

15   So I guess you could say that we laughed my mother
16 right through treatment. And she did great. Even loved it
17 when Dad wore a pink T-shirt in her honor. Every day for a
18 month. And when he shaved his head to match hers. We
19 bonded together in a way that just can't be described. It
20 was the worst and best thing we had ever gone through.

21   That's why when my mother finished treatment, I felt
22 like something more needed to be done. T-shirts and funny
23 memories just couldn't be enough to mark such a
24 momentous occasion. That's when I decided to get the
25 breast cancer sign tattooed on my ankle. For my mom.

26   I still wouldn't say that I'm a fan of tattoos, but I can
27 say that I finally *get* them. Sometimes you need a lifetime
28 reminder to be grateful. So this is for you. I love you, Mom.

65. Absentminded Should Not Equal Grounded

(Girl)

1   I think it's totally unfair that I'm grounded because I
2 forgot to text my mother when I got to my friend Nicole's
3 house. How can I be punished for being absentminded? It's
4 not like I didn't go where I said I was going; I just forgot to
5 "check in." How can that be a punishable crime?
6   She's such a hypocrite, too, because she forgets stuff all
7 the time. Just last week she forgot to pick me up after band
8 practice. I was there all by myself for over an hour because
9 she had her cell phone off and I couldn't get a hold of her.
10 Guess who Mr. Slone got mad at because he couldn't go
11 home until *all* the students were picked up? Me! I didn't see
12 her getting in trouble for that. But I'm pretty sure that's why
13 I dropped down a chair in my section this week.
14   And it wasn't that long ago that she completely forgot
15 to make my orthodontist appointment and so I had to keep
16 my braces on two extra months. That might not seem like
17 a lot to her, but it was an eternity to me. Just ask anyone
18 who is counting down the days until they get their braces
19 off. Waiting even one *day* longer is enough to make you
20 angry.
21   But the worst was a few years ago when she actually
22 forgot my birthday. That's right. My *mother* really and truly
23 forgot my birthday. All day went by and nothing. No
24 presents. No cake. No special dinner. I just kept waiting.
25 And waiting. Thinking it must be something big for her to
26 act so unaware, like maybe a surprise party or something.

1   But nothing.
2   When my grandmother called that night to wish me
3   happy birthday my mother finally got a clue. Tried to blame
4   it on a very hectic week at work and how her days were all
5   mixed up. But come on, no one forgets their kid's birthday.
6   I think I'll go remind her of that. If nothing else, she should
7   be able to see that it's her fault that I can't remember
8   anything. I'm just like her.

66. Not Cool, Dad

(Guy)

1   Some things just sound better than they ever really are.
2 Ask any kid if it wouldn't be cool to have a parent who's in
3 a band and they'd all be like, "Heck yeah!" And they'd
4 envision some great rock star who was rich and famous and
5 totally amazing. The kind of star that would make all your
6 friends envious and you the most popular kid in school. The
7 kind that would hold concerts in your backyard and every
8 kid would want to be invited.
9   That could've been my lot in life. If, number one, my
10 father was in an actual band that anyone had heard of, and,
11 number two, they played songs that weren't around when
12 my grandparents were born. My father's gig belongs on a
13 cruise ship or at minimum an old folks' Christmas party. Or
14 wedding.
15   It'd actually be OK that no one has ever heard of his
16 band except the fact that he always has to announce that
17 he is *in* a band. Why can't he keep that to himself? Can't he
18 see that my friends are *not* impressed with his seventies-
19 style sparkly track suit and teased out wig? Why can't he
20 just talk about his day job as an accountant?
21   The thing that really stinks is that my dad doesn't even
22 sound that bad. In fact, I'd even call him good. Great even.
23 He plays a pretty mean guitar, too. So why couldn't he have
24 been the kind of rock star that any kid would die to have as
25 a father? The kind who doesn't wear anything with a
26 rhinestone on it. You know what? I'd even settle for country
27 singing at this point. Not even rock and roll. Just anything
28 that doesn't sound like it belongs in an elevator.
29   Come on, Dad! Get a clue. You are *not cool!*

67. Taking It for Granted

(Girl or Guy)

1   There are some things in life you get so used to that
2 even though you don't mean to take them for granted, you
3 often do. For me, it was our annual Christmas lights van
4 ride. Every year on Christmas Eve we loaded up our van, all
5 dressed in our pajamas, to drive around and look at the
6 decorations and lights in all the different neighborhoods
7 around town. Mom would pack thermoses of hot chocolate
8 and snacks and we would stay out for hours. I remember
9 giggling over the fact that my father, who was always so
10 serious, actually drove around in his pajamas — out in
11 public!
12   I remember loving this as a child. Singing Christmas
13 carols. Staying up really late. The cherished candy that we
14 weren't normally allowed to eat. There was so much to love
15 about that night. Later, as a pre-teen, even though I tried to
16 act like I hated it, I really didn't. I complained enough to
17 hold up the act, but deep down, I wouldn't have missed it
18 for the world.
19   It wasn't until high school that I realized that something
20 so simple — a ride in a van — wasn't so simple after all. At
21 the beginning of my junior year, my father lost his job. And
22 though I know he did everything he could to find work, he
23 just wasn't getting anywhere. Mom was working a minimum
24 wage job, which after years of being a stay-at-home mom,
25 it was the best she could get.
26   That December when our van broke down, we didn't
27 have the money to fix it. Clearly, our annual pajama ride to
28 look at the lights was not going to happen. At least that's

1   what we thought. But on Christmas Eve night, our neighbor,
2   an elderly man we hadn't always paid the most attention to,
3   drove up with a rented van and said, "Look what I found.
4   Santa's sleigh. It's yours for the night!"
5   We didn't even know that he'd paid attention all those
6   years. I guess just like we hadn't really paid attention to
7   him. It made us all both very happy and very sad. That
8   night, Mr. Harris, pajamas and all, joined us on our annual
9   Christmas lights van ride, and he has every year since.

68. Pet Visitation

(Girl)

1   You know how in most families it's the kids that are
2 caught in the middle when their parents break up? Well, in
3 our case, it's not my sister and I, it's our dog. Princess. The
4 name should totally give it away that our dog is not your
5 average dog and has never been treated like the average
6 dog. It isn't even exaggerating to say that our dog is treated
7 better than anyone in the house. She has special food,
8 hand-knit sweaters, jeweled collars, and gets a manicure
9 more than most women do. She even has a special bed in
10 every room. That's right, my dog has more beds than
11 everyone in the house combined. To say that she totally
12 lives up to her name, Princess, is a major understatement.
13   It's not that I don't love her. We all do. She's completely
14 precious and loveable. Very good-natured and a great dog to
15 snuggle up on the couch with. But it is kind of insulting that
16 my parents are actually fighting over custody of the dog and
17 not us. It's become a real knock-down, drag-out fight over
18 who gets primary custody of Princess. Who gets her on the
19 holidays caused a screaming fight that lasted for hours.
20 There's no telling how much they've paid their lawyers over
21 just that one issue.
22   My dad sure didn't fight that hard to keep us. Mom
23 offered every other weekend and he took the deal in a
24 heartbeat. Didn't even try to get any nights during the week.
25 The dog, however, they want to split *exactly* even. One night
26 here. One night there. With a full-written agreement on
27 everything. Who pays for college isn't a bone of contention,
28 but who is responsible for Princess's vet bills sure is.

1   I guess in the long run, we should be happy that they
2 aren't fighting over us. They're fighting over a dog. We
3 should be happy, right?

69. The Price of Being Popular

(Girl)

1   I've got too many friends. Never thought I would say that
2 since being popular was my number one goal since I started
3 middle school. But with friends comes responsibility and
4 commitment and I'm out of time *and* money!
5   My friends seem to have problems twenty-four-seven. I
6 am constantly dealing with their drama and their issues. I
7 feel like a counselor on call. I never get a break. It doesn't
8 matter what time of day or night, they're texting me or
9 calling me. So and so said this. What does he mean by that?
10 What should I say to him? What should I say to her? It's
11 nonstop babble! I am having a hard time getting my
12 homework done. And I never have time to just chill. I can't
13 remember the last time I watched a movie or just sat in my
14 room listening to music.
15   Then there's the presents. For every friend comes a
16 birthday. And Christmas. And stupid other things like "last
17 day of school" or "first day of school." Having friends is
18 making me broke! Even though we set a five-dollar limit on
19 gifts, that's a lot of five dollars adding up. I can only babysit
20 so much. And I don't want to spend every dime I make on
21 my friends. Not that I don't like them enough to, but come
22 on, there are things that I need too.
23   So I think it's time to trim down the list. Maybe I need
24 a naughty and nice list like Santa. Only mine will be the gift
25 and no gift list. But how do I do that? How do I not buy a
26 present for someone that I know will buy me one? Would a

1 nice handmade card take the edge off? What if I get
2 everyone to institute a no-gift-giving rule? Then they would
3 think I was a Scrooge. Maybe I can just start a fight with
4 each one right around the time it's their birthday? Then
5 afterwards, I'll make up with them. It's the perfect plan. If I
6 do this right, I could have a gift-free birthday year. And by
7 the time Christmas rolls around, I might even have money to
8 buy each one of them a gift. And I won't have trimmed down
9 my list.

70. You're Small and I Love You

(Guy)

1   I grew up in Texas. The state where everyone knows that
2 bigger is better. Everything has to be big and people often
3 get caught up in trying to "one up" the other. It's probably
4 what started the biggest hamburger, biggest pizza, and
5 biggest sundae at all the local restaurants. And the
6 challenges that went with each. Most offered a free meal if
7 you could finish the biggest item they were offering. Oh, and
8 don't forget the picture to go with it.

9   I guess that's why I grew up believing that if something
10 was small, it wasn't really worthwhile. Not a cool thing to
11 believe when you're the shortest kid in the class. I kept
12 waiting for my growth spurt so that I could join the towering
13 boys in my class. Seemed like Texas was growing everyone
14 big, but me.

15   It wasn't until third grade that I got a different
16 perspective on small being better. It was Valentine's Day
17 and all of the kids had brought a gift for the teacher, Mrs.
18 Monroe. Now let me tell you something about Mrs. Monroe.
19 She was beautiful, inside and out. She was the nicest
20 person I'd ever met and all of us were in awe of her. That's
21 why I wanted to make sure I had the perfect gift for her.

22   I picked it out and my mom paid for a tiny little silver
23 necklace with a locket that wasn't bigger than a pea. For
24 some reason, it had caught my eye and I wouldn't have
25 anything but that. That day, though, when I saw Mrs.
26 Monroe opening big boxes of candy that got bigger and

1 bigger, I started to squirm in my seat. Maybe my gift was
2 too small.
3   Later when everyone was doing work at their desk, I
4 went up to Mrs. Monroe's desk and apologized for giving her
5 such a tiny little locket. "Are you kidding me?" she said. "I
6 absolutely love it!"
7   "But it's too small," I argued.
8   She smiled and shook her head. "You're small, and I love
9 you. Don't you know that sometimes the best things come
10 in tiny packages?"
11   I never forgot her telling me that. And from that day on,
12 I don't ever remembering wishing that I was bigger.

71. Paperboy

(Guy)

1 "It's a thankless job but somebody's got to do it."
2 That's what my father said the year he made me get a paper
3 route. He also added, "It'll teach you responsibility and grow
4 your character." He didn't even ask if I wanted to grow my
5 character. Which, let's face it, I didn't.
6 It sounds like an easy job, throwing papers on
7 everyone's front lawn, but it isn't. Especially when not
8 everyone gets a paper. That means you have to keep up
9 with who is a subscriber and who isn't. Otherwise, you have
10 to pay for the papers you give to the wrong houses by
11 mistake.
12 And you may not know this, but it's still *dark* when you
13 get your paper. Like pitch black dark, which means *not*
14 sunny and warm. My fingers are always numb by the end of
15 my route and that's with gloves on. And you may not stop
16 to think about this either, but sometimes it's *raining or*
17 *snowing* when you get your paper. Neither of the two make
18 for a great time, let me tell you. Either one means I have all
19 this pre-work I have to do in putting each paper in its own
20 little plastic bag. Which means I have to get up *even* earlier
21 than normal, which is *way* before a kid of any age should be
22 up.
23 The only cool thing about being up so early is seeing the
24 sun come up. Not too many kids my age get to see that on
25 a daily basis. It'd probably be safe to say that some of my
26 friends have never seen the sun come up. And probably
27 never want to. I know that I never would have if my dad
28 hadn't made me take this job. Of course I can never tell

1   anyone that. A guy that likes watching the sun rise is just
2   asking to get beat up.
3   There is one other plus about being a paper boy. My dad
4   was totally wrong about it being a "thankless job." You
5   wouldn't believe the tips I get! Maybe people really do
6   appreciate the fact that I'm up in the dark, rain, and snow,
7   delivering the paper to their door.

72. Choices

(Girl)

1   One day when I went to the mall with my friends I had
2 twenty dollars in my pocket and an endless list of things I
3 wanted to buy. The twenty wouldn't even come close to
4 covering it so I knew it would all come down to choices.
5 Which items were on sale and which ones could I really
6 afford to buy. My parents had ingrained in me the
7 importance of making the right choice since I was a very
8 little girl. They were all about choices and consequences.
9 There were no free rides around my house. No getting off
10 the hook if you broke a rule.
11   For example, if I chose not to clean my room when my
12 mom asked me, I not only had to clean my room later that
13 day, but I'd have an extra chore to do as well. If I chose to
14 back talk my dad about something, I lost my phone
15 privileges. And if I piled up my plate at a buffet line because
16 my eyes were bigger than my stomach, I was expected to
17 eat it all and not waste food. Pretty obvious that I was used
18 to choices and consequences my whole life.
19   But nothing prepared me for that day. On our way into
20 the mall, an elderly woman was situated at the entrance,
21 holding a sign asking for food or money. It didn't take a
22 genius to know that she was homeless. She was dirty and
23 frail and looked like she hadn't eaten a real meal in a long
24 time. I didn't even stop to give her a second glance as we
25 passed her, which is why I couldn't understand that
26 everywhere I looked I saw her face. In every store as I
27 searched for items that I wanted, her dark-shadowed eyes
28 kept popping into my mind.

1   About an hour later when we stopped at the food court
2 to get something to eat, I knew what I had to do. There was
3 a reason why I couldn't find just the right thing to buy that
4 day. Something kept holding me back. Something kept
5 saying, "You don't really need that, do you?" I stood in line
6 at the healthiest restaurant there was, not the burger place
7 like I would've chosen, and I bought the biggest combo of
8 chicken and rice they had. I added an extra side of fresh
9 steamed broccoli and a cup of hot coffee. Then, with my
10 friends watching in confusion, I walked the meal out to the
11 woman in front of the mall. I'll never forget the look of
12 gratitude on her face when I handed her the food.

13   My parents were right to teach me about choices and
14 consequences, but they also taught me about choices and
15 rewards. It was just a lesson I had forgotten.

73. Annoying Little Brother

(Guy)

1   Sometimes things happen for a reason even though it
2 might take you awhile to figure it out. That's what happened
3 to me a few years ago. Back when my baby brother was two-
4 years-old. He was so cute and totally annoying. He followed
5 me around like a little puppy, got in all my stuff, and often
6 would sneak into my room and sleep with me when he was
7 supposed to be learning to sleep in his own big boy bed.
8 Just like any big brother, I was completely annoyed by this
9 little being that would not leave me alone.
10   But there was one day he was particularly worse. He
11 would not leave my side. And to top it off it was my
12 birthday. Needless to say, every birthday photo had him in
13 it. There he was while I opened my presents. There he was
14 when Mom brought me my cake. The little booger even
15 helped me blow out my candles. So much for my special
16 day, because it all became about him. Let's face it, who's
17 going to steal the show? A cute toddler with icing on his
18 face or a pimply-faced twelve-year-old whose smile is so odd
19 it makes people uncomfortable? You know what I'm talking
20 about. Those awkward years when your teeth are too big for
21 your mouth and you can't quite get a real smile out.
22   Anyway, I remember going to bed pretty upset that
23 night. Swearing that I would never forgive him. Why had he
24 picked *that* day to be even more clingy than usual? And
25 then the unthinkable happened. My brother snuck out that
26 night and drowned in our neighbor's pool. It was the worst
27 moment of our lives.
28   A few weeks later, Mom stumbled upon her camera. In

1   an instant we all remembered how Adrian had been the
2   camera hog of the day. Little did we know that those
3   birthday photos would be the last we ever took of him. I
4   probably don't need to tell you that my family cherishes
5   every one. Especially me because I realize how lucky I was
6   to have him so close to me that day. I just wish I had known
7   to appreciate it more. It was the best birthday gift ever. I
8   just didn't know it.

74. Allergic?
I Don't Think So

(Girl or Guy)

1   I've been conducting a little experiment. Or maybe you
2 would consider it to be more of an undercover operation to
3 uncover the truth. See, all my life I've wanted a dog. Not
4 just any kind of dog, but an Alaskan husky with deep blue
5 eyes. I've wanted one for so long, I can't remember a time
6 when I wasn't obsessed with getting one. I've done my
7 research, too. Where to get one. The best food so that the
8 dog has the shiniest coat. And how much exercise it needs
9 to be healthy.
10 And I've promised a million times that I'll be completely
11 responsible for the dog. I will feed it, and walk it, and poop
12 scoop the yard. I know that every kid makes these promises
13 to their parents, but I really mean it and I've always been a
14 really responsible kid.
15 I guess that's why my parents knew they couldn't use
16 the whole you-won't-really-take-care-of-it excuse for me not
17 getting the dog. Oh no. They needed something better.
18 Something I couldn't argue. "Your dad's allergic," they told
19 me. And I believed them for a while. Several years in fact.
20 But then I started noticing things. Like that fact that when
21 we visited my uncle's house, who has three very large and
22 hairy dogs, my dad never sneezed. Or how we could go to
23 the pet store to buy new fish for our stupid aquarium and
24 even though I made Dad go to the puppy section, he still
25 never sneezed or coughed or got red eyes like my mom does
26 when it's ragweed season.

1   I started to feel duped. So I've taken it a step further. I
2   have to be sure before I confront them with the evidence. My
3   friend, Zack, has the same kind of husky I've always
4   wanted. I went to his house after school today and collected
5   a whole baggie full of dog hair. Guess where I put all that
6   hair? My dad's pillowcase. Tonight, we'll know one hundred
7   percent just how allergic my dad really is. Cross your fingers
8   that I'm right — otherwise I'm going to be in a whole lot of
9   trouble!

75. Halloween Horrors

(Girl or Guy)

1   My mother is completely out of control when it comes to
2   Halloween. Our house looks like a junkyard. She decorates
3   every inch of it. Tombstones, fake hands clawing the earth,
4   and an unlimited amount of ghosts hanging from every limb
5   on our trees. Then there are bats and spider webs and
6   skulls and witches. Absolutely anything ever made for
7   Halloween is sticking or hanging in our yard or on our house.
8   Everywhere you look is something creepy and ... tacky.
9   I didn't mind it so much when I was younger. Back then it
10   seemed cool that our house was the most decorated on the
11   street. Now it's just embarrassing. I'm sure everyone is
12   wondering what kind of devil-worshipping freaks must live
13   here. I've actually seen people circling the neighborhood
14   just because they need a second look. Who could blame
15   them? There's no way to take it all in the first time around.
16   She used to just decorate the outside. Maybe she was
17   trying to keep up with Mrs. Trammel? I don't know. But now
18   that she's covered the yard, front *and* back, she's moved to
19   decorating the inside, too. Why would anyone care that we
20   have ghost-shaped soap, I ask you? Or kitchen towels with
21   black cats with green jeweled eyes?
22   She has to take the whole week off work to get it done.
23   Five whole vacation days. Decorating. For Halloween.
24   Doesn't that seem a little crazy to anyone else? And the fact
25   that she does it the week after Labor Day? You know that's
26   in *September,* right?
27   I think we need to convince her she's a mummy and
28   wrap her up tight in a straight jacket. I'm serious! She
29   needs therapy. No one gets this obsessed over Halloween.

76. He'll Be Right Over

(Guy)

1   "He'll be right over." That's what my mother said to my
2   neighbor, old lady Hacker. She didn't even ask me. Just
3   volunteered me to go mow the woman's lawn. She sure is
4   free with offering my time for volunteering, which is funny
5   because I seem to recall that last month when Mrs. Hacker
6   called to ask Mom to volunteer at Friday night Bingo, Mom
7   was quick to say that she was too busy. Which was a lie
8   because all Mom did that night was sit on the couch
9   watching old movies.
10   Isn't there some kind of law about child labor? It's bad
11   enough that I have to mow *our* lawn. How can they make me
12   mow other people's, too? And for what? Fresh baked
13   cookies? Mom knows that Mrs. Hacker never pays me.
14   She's generous with her "thank yous" but not her money.
15   Believe me, I got my hopes up the first time I got
16   volunteered to shovel her sidewalk after a big snowfall. Do
17   you know how many hours I spent over there in the freezing
18   cold? The only thing that kept me going was the thought of
19   how much money she was sure to pay me. *Not.* I think that
20   time I got banana bread. And I'm allergic to bananas! They
21   make my tongue itch.
22   "Just think of it as a good deed," Mom tells me. "She's
23   old and all alone."
24   Fine. I get that. I even feel sorry for her, living all alone
25   in that big house. But come on, why am I the only one in the
26   family required to be charitable to her? I don't see anyone
27   else working for her for free. Or working for her at all! Next
28   time Mom lies to get out of helping her, I'm marching right

1   over there and telling Mrs. Hacker the truth. It's only fair
2   that if I have to volunteer, Mom does, too!

77. Grandma's Doll

(Girl)

1 My grandma has always been the sweetest person I've
2 ever known. She never has a mean thing to say about
3 anyone. I don't think I've ever seen her really mad about
4 anything. She is always calm and peaceful.

5 At least that's how she's always been. Lately, ever since
6 she got diagnosed with Alzheimer's, it's changed her. She
7 gets snappy over things that would never have bothered her
8 before and sometimes she yells at her dog, which she has
9 never done in her life. Not even the year he chewed a hole
10 in the wall.

11 I know it's the disease making her this way, but it
12 breaks my heart. She would be devastated to know that
13 she's acting like this. I guess that's one good thing about
14 being forgetful: She doesn't remember what she used to be
15 like, and she doesn't remember when she says or does
16 mean things now.

17 There's one thing that seems to help my grandma feel
18 better. It's an old doll that she gave me when I turned nine.
19 When she gave it to me, she also gave me a whole wardrobe
20 of handmade items for the doll to wear. I can't tell you how
21 many hours I've spent playing with that doll. Of course
22 those days were a long time ago. I hadn't even thought
23 about the doll for many years. Then one day when my
24 grandma was visiting me, she picked it up off my shelf and
25 told me how it was her favorite doll because her father had
26 given it to her when he came back from the war. I didn't
27 have the heart to tell her the truth, so I let her keep it. She
28 carries that doll around all the time now. And she has

1   memories that seem to give her peace, even if they aren't
2   real.
3   Even though the doll will one day be mine again,
4   probably to pass along to a daughter, I'll always think of it
5   as Grandma's Doll.

78. A Big Full Moon

(Girl)

1   There are reasons why I should never play sports. Such
2 as, I have big feet. I have *two* left feet. I have no balance. I
3 have no depth perception. I can't walk across the room
4 without getting out of breath. My feet smell when I wear
5 sneakers. I sweat too much. I get too thirsty. Activity makes
6 me cough.

7   But did that stop my parents from forcing me to take
8 tennis lessons and then join the tennis team? The team
9 that had so few people try out for it that they were forced to
10 take me? *No.* It did not stop any of that from happening.

11   Which is why I had the most embarrassing moment of
12 my life. Picture this. The buses are lined up for after-school
13 pickup right across from the tennis courts. They're full.
14 Ready to roll. A few car riders are walking by, including *the*
15 cutest boy in the seventh grade. The same cutest boy I'd
16 liked since the first day of middle school.

17   Maybe that's why I did it. I don't know. But for some
18 reason I decided that I needed to jump across the net to get
19 to the other side of the court. And that's when *it* happened.
20 My shorts got snagged at the top, and even though I landed
21 on the other side, kind of strung up on the net, my shorts
22 *did not.* That's right, I was giving a full moon to the entire
23 school! Including *the* cutest guy in the world. Worst part
24 was, everyone was laughing so hard, no one came to help
25 me! Not even the coach. I swear I was hung up there for five
26 minutes — or maybe a lifetime — I'm not sure which.

27   So maybe *now* my parents will believe me that I should
28 *not* play sports.

79. High Waters and Coke-Bottle Glasses

(Guy)

1   I am not the kind of guy who gets girlfriends. I know this
2 because I've never had a girlfriend my whole entire life. I
3 know you're looking at me and you're not surprised. Is it the
4 high waters or the coke-bottle glasses that convince you the
5 most? Or is it the striped pullover shirt or bowl cut hairdo?
6   I'm not oblivious to the reasons why I have stayed a
7 single man. And I could choose to change them. I could
8 even get contacts and get my hair feathered and highlighted
9 like some of the really cool guys do. I could even get my
10 mother to buy me new clothes instead of making me wear
11 my brother's hand-me-downs. I could even ask that she let
12 me pick them out instead of her. I *could* do all of those
13 things.
14   But I don't. I guess I'm kind of a romantic. I want a girl
15 to like me for me. For who I am on the inside, not what I
16 look like on the outside. It's crazy, I know. And clearly it's
17 not working since I can't even get a girl to notice me, much
18 less get to know the real me. But what if I did suddenly
19 transform into this really hot guy — don't laugh, it could
20 happen — and then all the girls did want to talk to me? How
21 would I know if it was real? If they really even cared about
22 me, or if they just wanted a hot guy to call their boyfriend?
23   It makes me think that beautiful people must have a
24 really hard time figuring out who their real friends are. I
25 wonder if they ever do. Maybe they go their whole lives
26 wondering if their looks are their only good quality? The only

1 thing that makes people attracted to them. I think that
2 would be sadder than being like me. All alone. Without a
3 girlfriend.
4   At least that's what I tell myself anyway.

80. Couples Only

(Girl or Guy)

1   You know how they make those stupid T-shirts that say,
2 "So and so went some place fabulous and all I got was this
3 crummy T-shirt?" Well, that's my life. My parents don't take
4 me anywhere.
5   "Couples only. Sorry, honey," they tell me as they jet off
6 to some other far off exotic place. Then, when they come
7 back, they have the nerve to show me their pictures as they
8 rave about how "fabulous" it all was. And they wonder why
9 I get mad? Who wouldn't? Listening to them go on and on
10 about how clear the water was, or how white the sand was,
11 or how awesome the food was is worse than the lame
12 souvenirs they bring me back. What does one really do with
13 a pair of maracas? Or, at last count, thirteen seashell
14 necklaces!
15   The absolute worst part is that they try to make it
16 educational. They make a big deal of showing me on the
17 globe exactly where they'll be and how many miles or hours
18 away that is and how I'll be freezing my butt off at
19 Grandma's house while they'll be toasty warm in a balmy
20 eighty-ish degrees!
21   It just isn't fair that I'm left behind every time. How
22 much trouble can I possibly be? I don't really eat that much.
23 In fact, I bet I could still order off the kid's menu. I've got
24 headphones, so they won't even have to talk to me. And if
25 they get me my own room, they won't even know I'm there.
26 Why can't they see that it's a win-win situation?
27   Oh, and by the way, Mom and Dad, taking me camping
28 once a year does not let you off the hook. I want beaches

1   with see-through water and white sand and coral and
2   colorful fish. Not a murky lake that looks like muddy
3   pudding. Come on, let's be fair about all this!

81. My Name Is Storm

(Girl)

1   When I was a little girl I used to get teased about my
2 name. "You're like the weather," the kids in kindergarten
3 would say. Not exactly cruel or even clever, but hey, they
4 were only five-year-olds. Their teasing was enough to make
5 me embarrassed and shy. I didn't speak a lot those first
6 years in school. In fact, I barely spoke at all.

7   But I guess my parents knew what they were doing when
8 they named me Storm, because just like a tropical storm
9 out at sea, things were brewing up inside of me. The
10 calmness on the outside did not reflect the turbulence
11 swelling up inside me. Looking back, it should've been easy
12 to see that a hurricane was coming.

13   All that quiet finally came to an end the year I turned
14 eleven. I'm not sure why. I don't remember a specific event
15 that triggered it. I just know that all of a sudden the silence
16 was over. In a brief moment, I became the most talkative,
17 outgoing student the teacher had ever seen. I wouldn't shut
18 up! At home. At school. Even in church! All those years of
19 sitting quietly were over.

20   I think I surprised myself even more than the others.
21 Who knew I had so much to say? The calm before the storm
22 was definitely over. It's freeing that I no longer care that my
23 name isn't normal like Allison or Mary. I'm happy that my
24 parents knew that I needed something unique. So if you're
25 someone like me, a kid with a name that you don't normally
26 find on a person, embrace it! You just never know what's
27 inside you, just waiting to come out.

28   Of course in that case, I just hope you aren't named
29 something like Bean, because that would be terrible!

82. Just Another New Year

(Girl)

1   So it's New Year's Day. Once again. And once again I've
2 spent way too many hours obsessing over what I need to
3 change for the new year. The dreaded resolutions. Should I
4 eat better, exercise more, be a better friend? Clean my room
5 more often so my mom and I won't fight as much? Or
6 maybe I should just be a better daughter in general? Of
7 course there's always the educational options. Read more.
8 Study more. Turn in my homework on time.
9   There's so much to consider. So many things that could
10 be improved. It's all so overwhelming. That's why I've
11 created a chart. With two columns: doable and the not-so-
12 doable. Because, let's face it, some things are just
13 downright impossible. Still, you have to consider all your
14 options. All the possible imperfections that you may want to
15 improve for the next year.
16   I figure I can do several from the doable column and
17 maybe only one from the not-so-doable column. Surely I can
18 take on one monumental task and see it through. This year
19 could be the one where I really follow through on what I say
20 I'm going to do. And not just in January either. I'll do it the
21 whole year. When I get to December next year, I won't have
22 anything to obsess over. My "improvement" list will be so
23 slim it won't even bother me that it's time for resolutions.
24   This is the year. I can feel it. The year of change. The
25 year of unbroken resolutions! The year of — (Pause, then look
26 to left) what? Clean my room now? Are you kidding me? It's
27 not even dirty! (Pause) Vacuum, too? But I just did that a
28 few weeks ago!

83. Cell Phone Blues

(Guy)

1   I think I am the only kid in middle school that doesn't
2 have a cell phone. I might even be the only kid in all of Scott
3 County that doesn't own a cell phone. My parents are so
4 old-fashioned. It's like they're stuck in the Seventies or
5 something. They think that just because they made it
6 through middle school without a phone, I can, too.

7   Can't they see how much easier life would be if I just
8 had a phone? They would always be able to get in touch with
9 me. And me with them! Like just last week when they
10 panicked because I didn't ride the bus home. They totally
11 forgot I was going home with Matt. My mom was hysterical
12 by the time she found me. Or what about the time when
13 they forgot track practice was over an hour earlier than
14 usual and I was the only kid still waiting at the school?
15 Don't they know how dangerous that is? I could've been
16 abducted!

17   And with the new technology, cell phones are
18 educational. I can access the Internet anywhere. That
19 means information is always at my fingertips. How can they
20 deprive me of knowledge like that? Not to mention all the
21 other helpful tools like tip calculator and GPS. And weather.
22 Don't forget that. If I had a phone I would know exactly how
23 to dress for school. No more days of wearing shorts when a
24 cold front is coming through. Or not having a hood when it's
25 going to rain. Just think if there's a tornado. Or an
26 earthquake. Or hurricane. Or worse — a tsunami.

27   OK. Maybe I got a little carried away there. Yeah, I *know*
28 we don't even live near the ocean. But just think if I did,

1   Google Maps could tell me.

2   Come on, Mom. Dad. Listen to reason! There's

3   absolutely *no* reason on earth why I shouldn't have a phone.

84. Horrible Hypocrites

(Girl)

1   My friends are a bunch of hypocrites. They tell lies all
2 the time, but now just because I told one stupid little lie
3 they aren't even talking to me. It wasn't even that big of a
4 deal. It's not like they can't trust me or anything. I was
5 trying not to hurt anyone's feelings. Can't they see that?
6   It all started when Carrie invited me over to her house.
7 Just me. Not Becca. So when Becca asked where I was
8 going to be on Friday night, I couldn't tell her Carrie's house
9 or she would've been hurt. I didn't want Carrie mad at me
10 for telling, so I told Becca I was going to Marcy's house.
11 Becca doesn't like Marcy so I figured that wouldn't hurt her
12 feelings about not being invited. It was a perfect plan. And
13 completely harmless.
14   So then Becca tells Carrie that I'm staying over at
15 Marcy's house on Friday night and Carrie thinks that I'm
16 going to ditch her for Marcy. Even though I wasn't. So she
17 invites Becca to spend the night instead of me. When I try
18 to clear things up, Becca gets mad that I lied to her about
19 where I was really going and Carrie thinks that I'm still lying
20 and that I really was going to ditch her for Marcy.
21   What a mess! I was bound to get in trouble no matter
22 what I did. Because if I *had* told Becca the truth in the first
23 place, she would've been mad that she wasn't invited and
24 Carrie would've been mad that I told Becca when she asked
25 me not to. This is really *all* Carrie's fault because she knows
26 that the three of us always do everything together.
27   But not anymore apparently, because they won't even
28 look at me now. Maybe I'm better off this way. At least I

1   won't have to lie again. The next time someone invites me
2   over, if that ever happens again, I'm saying *no!* It's just way
3   too much trouble.

85. Santa Claus Isn't Coming to Town ... Anymore

(Guy)

1   I can't believe my parents led me on like this. And my
2   older brother, too? I thought he was cool. I never thought
3   they'd hide something as life changing as *this*. This isn't the
4   type of thing you're supposed to hear from friends,
5   especially not in middle school. Their words hit me like a
6   train. "You *still* believe in Santa? You know he's not real,
7   right?"

8   What did they mean? All fourteen years of my life I've
9   been a strong believer in the old jolly fat man. If he wasn't
10 real, then who eats all the cookies and milk I put out, and
11 brings me extra presents? And how can they explain the
12 reindeer tracks in my front yard? Not to mention, I always
13 get the gifts that were on the letter I sent to the North Pole.
14 It's not like my parents could pull all of that off.

15 Maybe my friends are wrong, and I'm right. I do have all
16 As, even in math. Plus in third grade, I was in a fourth grade
17 class. That counts for something, right? My friends don't
18 read at a tenth grade level, but I do. Maybe they're just not
19 smart enough to realize Santa's magical powers ... You
20 know, now that I'm hearing my own thoughts, maybe they
21 are right. How can one man travel the world in one night?
22 And how do elves know who's been good or bad? Johnny, a
23 boy in my third period language arts class, is always bad
24 and mean, and he always gets the best presents. If Santa
25 were real, shouldn't he give Johnny coal?

26 So yeah, I've realized that Santa Claus isn't real. But

1   now I know who really brings my extra gifts and eats the
2   milk and cookies. It's not my parents who are responsible,
3   or Santa's fake elves. It's got to be those sneaky little fairies
4   that are doing it. They're the fast ones!

86. Cat Lady

(Girl)

1   I know everyone has lame nicknames in middle school.
2 Four-eyes, Bookworm, things like that. But mine's the
3 worst. Worse than any nicknames you'll ever hear. Worst
4 than the worst nickname you could ever even imagine! It
5 hurts me to even say it or think about it. They call me ...
6 Cat Lady.
7   You see, I've loved cats my whole entire life. I've never
8 not had a cat living in my house for as long as I can even
9 remember. They're loyal, soft, and they're just so darn cute.
10 Everyone thinks I'm weird because I prefer precious kitties
11 over ugly, drooling dogs. Well, does their dog sleep with
12 them every night and cuddle with them all the time? At least
13 cats are lovable and don't leave me a mess in the yard to
14 clean up constantly.
15   Anyway, on the first day of my sixth grade year, I was
16 asked to write a poem about my favorite thing in the whole
17 world and present it in front of my language arts class. I
18 wrote mine about my cats. I put a lot of hard thought, love,
19 and memories into my poem. I was so excited to share it
20 with my classmates and friends.
21   As the teacher asked for volunteers, of course my hand
22 was raised higher than anyone else's, and I got picked to go
23 first. I walked proudly to the front of the room and read my
24 poem with confidence and a huge grin. As soon as I
25 finished, the worst moment of my life happened. The
26 popular boys started chanting, "Cat Lady, Cat Lady, Cat
27 Lady" over and over again! Then everyone else joined in. I
28 was humiliated.

1   To this day, I'm known as Cat Lady. I even heard a
2 teacher call me that before. My love for cats should have
3 been kept a secret. Why couldn't I be Four-eyes or
4 Bookworm? I just hope this nickname is forgotten before
5 high school ...

87. New Pool, New Friends

(Guy)

1   It took years and years of long, hard begging, but my
2 brother and I finally did it. We convinced our parents to get
3 us a brand new pool. We were both so excited and ready.
4 This meant lots of pool parties, midnight swims, and, best
5 of all, popularity! As soon as I started to spread the news
6 about our new pool around school, everyone, and I mean
7 *everyone,* wanted to come over to swim and try it out. Even
8 the popular people who didn't even know my name!

9   As soon as school let out for summer vacation, my
10 brother and I had tons of people over to swim in our pool
11 every single day. We would all do jumping competitions,
12 play basketball in the pool, and do diving tricks. I was on
13 top of the world and I thought nothing was going to bring
14 me down. Then, the most unimaginable thing *ever*
15 happened. As I was running to jump into the pool, I tripped
16 over a squirt gun and really hurt my leg. My parents rushed
17 me to the emergency room as soon as it happened, and
18 that's where they broke the horrible news to me.

19   "Your leg is broken."

20   "What? I think you have the wrong patient. It's only the
21 middle of the first week of summer, my leg can't be broken.
22 How will I be able to get in the pool and have all my new
23 friends over?"

24   The doctor didn't seem to care about my pool dilemma,
25 as he put me in a full-leg cast. For six whole weeks, my
26 social life went down the drain. Everyone still came to the
27 pool, yet they all came to see my brother. They didn't even
28 pay attention to me. Just splashed right in the pool. My

1 friends completely forgot about me, just because I couldn't
2 get in the water. I couldn't believe they had the nerve to
3 show their un-loyal faces at my house!
4   But they better just wait till I get out of this cast. I'll
5 have new friends over to swim in winter, if I have to.

88. Picked Last in Gym Class

(Guy)

1   I'm on the school's softball team, and I'm one of the star
2 players. I ran on the track team for school last year, and I
3 was the fastest. I'm friends with almost everyone around
4 and everything. Yet every time gym class comes around, I'm
5 picked last. After Douglass, the boy with glasses *and* the
6 skinniest legs known to man. In fact, most kids call him
7 Twigs. I even get picked after Glenna, the girl who never
8 takes her nose out of a book for enough time to notice we're
9 even in gym class.
10   Last week, we played softball. I'm on the school's
11 softball team. That's *my* sport! But I just stood there and
12 waited until, again, my name was said last. Dead last. Not
13 even second to last. I mean, maybe I could feel a little, tiny
14 bit OK about myself if I was at least *second* to last. Maybe
15 they forgot about me. That has to be the reason. I'm not one
16 of those lame kids who get picked last because they're a
17 nerd or not cool or something. That just absolutely can *not*
18 be me!
19   Maybe it's because I'm so good at sports they're
20 intimidated. I won't lie. I can throw a baseball really hard
21 and really fast and kick the ball in the goal almost every
22 time when we play soccer. Plus, when we play basketball, I
23 make at least one three-pointer each game! I'm even almost
24 as good as some of the athletic guys who are on the school
25 football team. They probably pick people like Douglass
26 before me to make him feel better about himself. It can't be

1 because I'm bad! Even the gym teacher compliments my
2 skill some of the time. That's a ton of proof right there.
3   I think everyone is just extremely jealous of my sports
4 skills. Or they feel bad for the other team, so they want
5 them to get a good player like me, so they try to let the
6 opposite team pick me. Yes, that's it! Both the teams are
7 just trying to be nice. Now that I know I'm such a big asset,
8 maybe gym class isn't so bad after all.

89. The Lunch Situation

(Girl or Guy)

1   The first day of school is so exciting, especially so I can
2 finally start my eighth grade year. The year I've been waiting
3 on since like fifth grade! New teachers, new classes, you
4 don't have to walk in lines anymore, not to mention the
5 freedom that comes with being the oldest kids in school!
6 There's only one thing that I'm really scared of. Actually,
7 terrified would be a much better word. The lunch situation.
8   I know it has to go through every eighth grader's mind.
9 I can't be alone in this fear. What if I walk into the lunch
10 room and I don't have anyone to sit with? Last year, I had
11 to eat lunch with brand new people. I didn't have one single
12 friend to sit with me. I was such a loner. I had to sit with all
13 the band geeks. I had to listen to them talk about the new
14 music they were learning in band and about how they
15 needed new mouthpieces, which was *so fun* — that can't
16 happen to me again this year. Not my last year in middle
17 school. I absolutely *have* to have friends to sit with at lunch.
18   What if I try to sit with some people and they tell me not
19 to sit with them, or that their table's full? My life would be
20 completely ruined! I'd have to move to a new school just to
21 avoid the humiliation. Or what if I have to sit all alone,
22 completely by myself? I'd rather eat in a bathroom stall, or
23 with a teacher, for goodness sakes! Hopefully the counselor
24 was kind to me this year when deciding which lunch to
25 assign me. Maybe all of my friends will have the same lunch
26 as me. If not, my mom is *going* to transfer me to a new
27 school, or even homeschool me. Where you sit at lunch may
28 not be the most important part of school, but it's a huge
29 deal.

90. Kisses from My Mommy

(Guy)

1   Everyone saw it. Even the sixth graders. Every single
2 person. The absolute worst day of my entire life. The end of
3 my life, actually. I will *never* live this down. I'll be getting
4 made fun of until I'm eighty years old. And it all happened
5 in two seconds. The blink of an eye. My mom had the nerve
6 to kiss me good-bye. In front of everyone! And the worst
7 part about it? Right smack-dab on the middle of my lips.

8   Now, I like to think of myself as a ladies' man. I text at
9 least five girls on an average day. I've already kissed two
10 girls and I'm only fourteen! So this ... incident, I guess you
11 could call it, is going to ruin my player reputation. No girl is
12 going to date a "mamma's boy."

13   I just *had* to miss the bus, didn't I? This never would've
14 happened if Mrs. McCandless hadn't assigned so much
15 homework. I stayed up so late trying to finish it; I couldn't
16 even wake up this morning to actually catch the bus. That's
17 why my mom had to drive me to school. And she just *had*
18 to wear bright red lipstick. Why couldn't she have just
19 skipped the makeup today?

20   Not only did everyone see her kiss me on my soft, lady-
21 kissing lips, but even after, I had to wear her lipstick all day!
22 No matter how long I spent in the bathroom scrubbing and
23 scrubbing at the bright red stain, it stayed put. Thanks for
24 that, twenty-four-hour-stay-put-lipstick.

25   Why me? Guys like me don't kiss their parents, let alone
26 even acknowledge their existence. We text girls and act cool.
27 And getting kissed by your mom ... that's definitely not
28 cool. I'll be lucky if anyone ever talks to me again. I'll be that

1   one guy who's going to be single until the day he dies. All
2   because of my mom. I think this deserves the silent
3   treatment ...

91. Teacher Crush

(Girl)

1   Gorgeous deep blue eyes. Tan skin. A voice that could
2 put a baby peacefully to sleep in a matter of seconds. This
3 is my fourth hour teacher, Mr. Layton. He used to be an
4 Abercrombie & Fitch model. How am I supposed to get any
5 work at all done in this class? My mom always gets onto me
6 for having a bad grade in his class, but she doesn't
7 understand what it's like in there. Every time he talks, I get
8 in a trance, and can't focus on anything but his perfectly
9 shaped face.
10   Everyone in school thinks I'm totally weird because of it.
11 I even broke up with my last boyfriend because of my
12 teacher. But it's not my fault. Blame him. He's so perfect
13 it's not fair. He makes pre-algebra my favorite subject,
14 when I actually hate math. I never want to leave his class. I
15 could just stare at him all day. I don't even blink so that I
16 don't miss anything.
17   Every day I look forward to going to his class. I even got
18 the nickname Teacher's Pet because everyone thinks I suck
19 up to him. But how could I not?
20   My mom says it's just a crush, but it's not. It's more. I
21 think I might love this man. But I'm not going to be the
22 weird girl who loves her teacher. I've seen the movies;
23 everyone thinks those girls are crazy and try to avoid them
24 as much as possible. I can't be one of them. I may love him,
25 but a girl needs a social life. He's worth the failing grade,
26 but definitely not worth not having any friends. You know,
27 now that I think about it, I may not love him. Maybe mom's
28 right about the crush thing ...

92. My Future as a Hairdresser...Family Style

(Girl)

1   It takes me two whole hours to fix my mess of a head of
2 hair into something manageable. My parents and sisters say
3 it looks like prom hair. You'd think that that would be a
4 good thing, right? Well, you're wrong. Apparently my hair
5 looks so good, that my mom wants me to do her hair every
6 morning, along with my two sisters. Talk about needy!

7   I don't know how they expect me to have enough time
8 to work on their hair. I can't lack on my style, that's just
9 not an option. Just the other day, my mom parades into my
10 room, in the midst of me working my magic onto my long
11 head of hair, and she asks me to stop what I'm doing to
12 "help" her fix her hair. I know "help" means start
13 completely over and make it look amazing. The nerve she
14 has!

15   I'm thinking I need to have an at-home class for them,
16 or even start charging for my services. I could get a lot of
17 money out of this. Ha! As if they'd actually pay me. Come
18 on, how hard is it to curl your hair? According to my sister,
19 it's impossible and I *have* to do it for her. Maybe if I started
20 not doing anything to my hair and wearing it the same every
21 day, they'd think I'd lost the touch and find someone else
22 to do it. Anyone else!

23   It's not that I mind doing it for them; it's just the fact
24 that they get credit for my work. When people see the
25 masterpiece I've created on the top of their head, they don't
26 automatically think, "Oh, I bet her sister did that for her."

1   Or what if their hair looks better than mine? I think the only
2   solution to this problem is to stop trying. I'll do it ... one day
3   ... maybe.

93. Boxers Are Not Appropriate for Assemblies

(Guy)

1   You know that bad dream you always have? The one that
2   you dread having just because it's so embarrassing to even
3   think about? The one where you're in your underwear in
4   front of the whole school? In my case, it's no longer just a
5   bad dream. Yes, this actually happened to me. And yes, it's
6   as horrible as it sounds.

7   It all started on my first day in gym class. We were
8   playing dodgeball, so we all headed to the locker rooms to
9   change into our shorts and T-shirts. When we started
10   playing dodgeball, I was on fire. I dodged every single ball
11   that was thrown my way and got at least ten people out.
12   Everyone thought I was the best, and I loved it. All the girls
13   were cheering me on, and the guys were patting me on the
14   back and yelling things like, "Nice dude." I had never had
15   this much encouragement. This was going to be the best
16   class of the year.

17   After the game, I headed back to the boys' locker room.
18   As I walked in, all the guys were high-fiving me, and telling
19   me how awesome I did. See, I'm not a popular guy, so
20   having all the guys telling me I was good at something was
21   like a dream come true.

22   I had gotten sweaty playing, so I took a quick shower.
23   As I got dressed, I noticed something. My pants were not
24   where I left them. I searched everywhere looking for them,
25   and nothing! How could this happen?

26   I walked out, hoping no one would see, to go to the

1   teacher to get some hand-me-down pants. As I walked out,
2   my life shattered. Apparently, there was an assembly being
3   held for the *whole entire* seventh grade. All I was wearing
4   was my T-shirt and boxers.
5   As soon as I walked out, all eyes were on me. It took two
6   seconds for all of the bleachers to be roaring with laughter.
7   Either this was a prank, or someone mistook my pants for
8   theirs. Either way, my nightmare had become reality!

94. I Can Be Rachel

(Girl)

1   I've always wanted to be one of them for as long as I can
2 remember. They have the most perfect hair. Their nails are
3 always manicured and un-chipped. They have guys drooling
4 all over them, and they have so many friends, they can't
5 even count them all. They're the popular girls. It's not that
6 I don't have friends, I do. But not like them.

7   So when I found an invitation to Megan Reece's party
8 stuffed into my locker, I was ecstatic. She's the most
9 popular girl in school! Even the eighth graders know who
10 she is, and we're only in seventh grade.

11   When she has a party, she goes all out. Limos, gift
12 baskets, famous bands, even cakes the size of my room.
13 I've always heard about her parties, and I've always
14 imagined myself actually going to one. But now that I've
15 been invited, there are so many things to think about. How
16 was I going to wear my hair? What outfit should I wear?
17 Better yet, I should just go buy a totally new outfit. New
18 shoes, dress, and, of course, accessories. After this party,
19 everyone will know who I am. There will probably even be
20 boys there, too. This will be my first boy-girl party. This is
21 going to be epic.

22   No more being an unknown, smarty pants. Now I'll be
23 one of them! I might even scrapbook the invitation. Cool
24 people scrapbook, right? I may even laminate ... wait.
25 What's that say? It says Rachel. The name on the invitation
26 says Rachel. But my name's Liz ... oh no! She must have
27 accidentally slipped this in my locker. Rachel's locker is two
28 down from mine.

1   I should put it back ... I should ... but I wonder ... do you
2   think she'd even notice if I went? Maybe she'd forget who
3   she actually invited ... I could still go. I could still be popular.

95. Superstar

(Girl)

1   When I was younger, I did a commercial. I was only like
2 five, but that commercial was internationally aired. It was
3 huge! I was known everywhere for it. Then I come into sixth
4 grade, expecting to be praised for my work, and, of course,
5 known for my fame, but I'm getting treated like a normal
6 student.

7   Apparently it's no big deal that I was a child star. I tell
8 my classmates, and I get the unworthy response of, "So?"

9   *So!?* This is a huge deal. I'm sure none of them have ever
10 starred in a commercial or anything like it. If they had, I
11 know I wouldn't be getting this sort of treatment. Their
12 parents should've taught them some respect when they're
13 in the presence of a big star like myself.

14   My teachers don't care either. I was expecting
15 homework passes, time extensions on my projects,
16 anything. But they treat me like a student. Like a boring,
17 normal student. They must be crazy to think *I'm* normal. I'm
18 a star. A celebrity. I'm more famous than anybody at that
19 whole school. I deserve the royal treatment.

20   I'm tempted to bring a video of my commercial to
21 school. Then it would get the attention it deserves, and I
22 would be appreciated for my starlike qualities. Everyone
23 would be so amazed by my performance, they would
24 immediately start treating me the way I deserve. I wouldn't
25 be sitting all alone at lunch.

26   You know what? I think I just figured out what to do for
27 my English project. It's perfect, really. I'll show the video as
28 part of a study on foreign films. Who says a commercial

1   can't count? It has just as much of a storyline as some of
2   these stupid classic books we read. That will remind these
3   nobodies just who I am.

96. Teacher's Least Favorite

(Girl or Guy)

1   I've been late to class once. I always do my homework with
2   one hundred percent effort and even turn it in on time. I'm
3   considered a model student in all of my other classes. But
4   then third period rolls around. My least favorite class of the
5   day. Of my whole entire school experience, actually.
6   Everything I do in that class is wrong and it's all because my
7   teacher hates me.
8   Ever since day one, she picked me out as her enemy.
9   Every time I answer a question, it's wrong. Even if the kid next
10 to me answers the same exact thing, just worded a little bit
11 differently than mine. That kid gets praised; I get mocked or
12 stared at like I've just said the most stupid answer on earth.
13   Every time I walk into class, she gives me this look. I
14 guess you could call it a death glare. It's like she doesn't even
15 want me to be in her class. The other day, I turned in a
16 homework assignment, and she gave me a zero because I
17 used a blue pen instead of a pencil. How is that even close to
18 being fair? I could be failing the seventh grade just because of
19 her.
20   My mom thinks I'm just making excuses because I have
21 a bad grade in her class. But that's just not the case. The fact
22 of the matter is that my teacher hates me and is out to get
23 me. My mom just doesn't want to believe it. She says
24 teachers don't pick favorites or hate any of their students. Well
25 man, is she wrong! You can't make this stuff up. I'm only
26 halfway through the year, and I already can't wait to get to the
27 eighth grade so I can be rid of her.
28   Teachers don't hate their students. *Ha!* Tell that to Mrs.
29 Penn!

97. Grounded

(Girl or Guy)

1   I've been home all weekend. I haven't seen my friends, or
2   even people for that matter, for two whole days. I think being
3   grounded for two weeks is a little extreme. All I did was come
4   in five minutes past my curfew.

5   OK, maybe it was an hour or two. But still, two weeks?
6   Come on. What's wrong with that? My friends' parents let
7   them get away with everything. Even stuff like detentions.
8   My mom would freak if I ever brought home a pink slip. Talk
9   about grounded for life! My parents are so strict. They have
10   rules for just about everything under the sun. Even the way
11   I eat. I always hear "No elbows on the table" or "Chew with
12   your mouth closed." They are *so* in my business *all* the time!

13   Groundings are just so pointless. I don't even learn
14   anything! I just sit in my room and sleep. They think that's a
15   punishment, but I actually need all the sleep I can get. And
16   it's time away from them, too. Peace and quiet, if you ask me.

17   At least I'm not grounded from my phone, like usual.
18   Now that's pure torture. I miss out on all the juicy stuff
19   going on with my friends. Friends who get to go do stuff on
20   the weekends because their parents *don't* ground them.
21   Ever! I can't wait until I'm old enough to move out. Then I
22   won't have all these stupid rules. I'll do what I want, when I
23   want, and for as long as I want. *No one* will tell me what to
24   do. I'll be free from all these restrictions. And when I have
25   kids, I'll remember how this feels and I'll let my kids do
26   whatever they want. My house will be the cool house. No
27   rules. No bedtimes. No curfews. No manners! Just *fun, fun,*
28   *fun!*

98. Band Geek

(Guy)

1   Lessons, jazz band, and marching band practice. That's
2 my whole entire life. No time for friends after school or even
3 time to watch just one episode of my favorite show. I'm like
4 two seasons behind on everything. It's not like I imagined
5 how my middle school years were going to go. But I can't
6 tell my mom that. Apparently I have a bright future in music
7 in her mind.

8   I'm not even that good. I'm fourth chair out of six. That's
9 not even halfway good! And I play the worst instrument in
10 the whole band. The trombone. It's not even something cool
11 like the saxophone. Or drums. At least then I could be
12 proud to be a band geek. But trombone? Come on. Have you
13 ever heard of a hot trombone player? Exactly.

14   At school, the band geeks aren't cool. At all. We're like
15 bottom of the food chain. The first ones to be picked on.
16 We're the kids with the shirts that say, "My mom thinks I'm
17 cool." Hahahaha.

18   Some of my bandmates do take it a little too far. Band
19 is their whole life. They eat, sleep, and breathe music. It's
20 all they ever talk about. Like seriously, they can't hold a
21 conversation about anything. It all comes back to music and
22 band. And they act like we're rock stars or something. At
23 least I have enough common sense to know we're only in
24 middle school band.

25   But even with all that, I guess being a band geek isn't
26 so bad. There's band camp and school band trips. Those
27 are always a lot of fun. We got to miss a week of school for
28 national competition last year. Plus state recognition for

1   being the number one middle school band is pretty
2   awesome. We're in the newspaper all the time. I guess when
3   you think about it, me and my band geek friends are just
4   about the most famous people at school!

99. Awkward

(Girl)

1   OK, I know everyone goes through an awkward stage.
2   But I'm pretty sure my awkward stage has lasted far too
3   long. It started in sixth grade ... Now I'm in eighth. Most
4   girls go through it fast. Then they come out of it looking like
5   beauty queens, with their perfect hair and smiles. They even
6   wear makeup!
7   See, I've tried the whole makeup thing. I think it just
8   makes my zits stand out more. And the perfect hair and
9   smile? Try braces and flat, straight hair every day. I don't
10 even know how to use a curling iron. I'm the girl who's six
11 feet tall and every time elderly people see me, they go on
12 and on about how I should play basketball and have a career
13 in it. Except for I couldn't make a shot if my life depended
14 on it. And dribbling? Forget it. I barely walk without tripping
15 now. Add a ball to the mix and it'd be over!
16   Of course my mom says I'm beautiful, but I'm not going
17 to parade around bragging about what my mom thinks of
18 me. Her opinion couldn't matter less in my school.
19 Especially to the boys.
20   They all fawn over the girls who aren't awkward like me.
21 That leaves me with the even more awkward boys, whose
22 voices haven't even changed yet, chasing after me. And
23 might I add, they're all about two feet shorter than me.
24 Awesome, right?
25   I just hope this awkward stuff doesn't last too much
26 longer. All of my brothers and sisters grew out of it really
27 fast, so maybe I will too. Except my mom went through it
28 long into college. That's right. College! At least that's what

1   I gather by looking at her old pictures. I sure hope I take
2   after my dad because I can't survive many more years of
3   this.

100. The Pants

(Girl)

1   It started out as a really good day, seemed pretty
2 normal. No fights with my dad as he drove me to school. I
3 didn't oversleep, which happens more than you'd think, and
4 I had the cutest outfit picked out to wear to school. As soon
5 as I walked in through the doors, my friends were
6 complimenting me left and right about how much they liked
7 my adorable outfit. They all said they were so jealous and
8 wished that they had my outfit. I was so excited. The day
9 was going perfect. That was until it happened.

10   As I bent over to pick up a pencil I dropped, I heard an
11 awful sound. The sound I never want to hear. Ever again.
12 *Riiiip!* It was the sound of my pants ripping right down the
13 middle. I had hoped no one noticed and prayed that no one
14 would until I could change them. But that's the complete
15 opposite of what happened.

16   One of my friends instantly screamed out, "You have a
17 huge rip in the back of your pants!" Just my luck. After she
18 said that, the whole class busted into laughter. I had people
19 coming up to me asking if they could take a picture on their
20 phone so they could post it. It's bad enough having the
21 whole class laugh at me, I can't even imagine the whole
22 cyber world joining in, too. I just hope I got to my locker in
23 time to tie my jacket around my waist before anyone got a
24 picture.

25   This would be the day I decide to wear my sunflower
26 underwear. That just made the whole situation more
27 hilarious for everyone else and more humiliating for me. The
28 whole way to the office I got pointed and laughed at. Could

1   this day get any worse? Apparently it could. When I called
2   my mom, she couldn't leave work to bring me different
3   pants. I had to borrow lost and found bright pink sweatpants
4   that were three sizes too big. So long, perfect day, I knew
5   you wouldn't last.

101. Smelly Cast

(Girl or Guy)

1   I always thought having a cast would be really cool. I
2 was the only one in my family to never have a broken bone.
3 I guess it was to be expected in a family full of athletes. But
4 seeing all the attention my brothers and sister always got
5 had made me kind of jealous. And even though they
6 complained when they had theirs, I really didn't see the
7 downside. Just seemed like a lot of whining about nothing.
8   And then I got mine. It was pretty cool at first. Everyone
9 was so helpful and nice about it. My friends carried my
10 backpack and books to and from class. My counselor had a
11 scribe follow me around to write for me and I got extensions
12 on all my homework assignments since I had to write left-
13 handed. Life was pretty good. For about a week. Then it all
14 went downhill.
15   First came the itching. Smack-dab in the middle of my
16 cast where I couldn't get to it. No matter what I stuck down
17 that thing — even though I was told repeatedly by my mom
18 not to put *anything* down in my cast. Did you know a small
19 itch is like *torture* to a person when they can't actually
20 scratch it? It's enough to make you go crazy! I wanted to
21 scream.
22   Then came the less-than-helpful attitude of my friends.
23 Apparently helping out a friend has a very short time limit.
24 I was barely into the second week when all of a sudden *no*
25 *one* was around to help carry my backpack or books.
26   The last straw is the smell. It is completely horrible. No
27 one wants to sit by me because of the odor wafting out from
28 my cast. It's disgusting. And unfortunately, I can't get away

1   from it. It literally makes me lose my appetite it's so awful.
2   I really don't think I can take three more weeks of this.
3   So, take it from me, the next time you're jealous and
4   you think someone has something you want — be very
5   careful what you wish for!

102. Mani-Pedi Girls

(Girl)

1   Everyone knows them. You know, the girls with their
2   nails and toenails always manicured and pedicured
3   perfectly. The mani-pedi girls. Well, those girls are my best
4   friends. They don't even go a week without getting them
5   redone. They always have the cute little designs on them,
6   too. I love it when they get the jewels on their big toes. Or
7   when they have flowers airbrushed on top of the main color.
8   It's so cute. I'm totally jealous, because my mom is way too
9   cheap to buy me a manicure or a pedicure.

10   She says I'm too young and that it's a waste of her
11   money to buy me fake nails that don't even last. I don't
12   know what she's talking about. How are they a waste of
13   money? They're actually very practical. And they last for
14   weeks. Maybe even months if you don't mind having a little
15   space at the back as they grow out. They're strong, too.
16   Much stronger than real ones. They help you peel off
17   stickers easier and clean gunk out of cracks and stuff. And
18   they look good, too. Much better than my chewed-up nails
19   ever could.

20   My mom just doesn't see this side of them. She only
21   sees that they're a lot of money. She says the fake glue-on
22   nails are just as good. You know, the ones that cost like
23   three dollars and pop off two seconds after you glue them
24   on. They aren't even close to the real thing.

25   How can she possibly expect me to be seen in those?
26   What if one of them pops off in front of everyone and my
27   secret is revealed? I'd never live that one down. And my
28   friends would probably think I'm cheap or something.

1   Thank goodness winter is coming. I'll just wear gloves
2 all the time so no one can see how hideous my nails are.

About the Author

This is Rebecca Young's seventh drama book for teens. Many of the monologues and plays she writes have been inspired by real life family or friend events — you'll have to guess which ones!

Ms. Young lives with her husband (Frank), two daughters (Kristina and Ashley), and two cats. Her family recently expanded to include a new cat (who was found up in a tree) and a new son-in-law named Chris (who was found by her daughter, Heather).

Whether you are an actor or a writer, she suggests this anonymous quote as a daily mantra: "You aren't finished when you lose; you are finished when you quit."

Never give up hope.

Order Form

Meriwether Publishing Ltd.
PO Box 7710
Colorado Springs, CO 80933-7710
Phone: 800-937-5297 Fax: 719-594-9916
Website: www.meriwether.com

Please send me the following books:

_____ **102 Monologues for Middle School Actors** $17.95
#BK-B327
by Rebecca Young
Including comedy and dramatic monologues

_____ **101 Monologues for Middle School Actors** $16.95
#BK-B303
by Rebecca Young
Including duologues and triologues

_____ **Famous Fantasy Character Monologs** $16.95
#BK-B286
by Rebecca Young
Starring the Not-So-Wicked Witch and more

_____ **100 Great Monologs #BK-B276** $15.95
by Rebecca Young
A collection of monologs, duologs and triologs for actors

_____ **102 Great Monologs #BK-B315** $16.95
by Rebecca Young
A versatile collection of monologues and duologues for student actors

_____ **Ten-Minute Plays for** $17.95
Middle School Performers #BK-B305
by Rebecca Young
Plays for a variety of cast sizes

_____ **More Ten-Minute Plays for** $17.95
Middle School Performers #BK-B319
by Rebecca Young and Ashley Gritton
Plays for a variety of cast sizes

These and other fine Meriwether Publishing books are available at your local bookstore or direct from the publisher. Prices subject to change without notice. Check our website or call for current prices.

Name: _____ email:_____

Organization name: _____

Address: _____

City: _____ State: _____

Zip: _____ Phone: _____

❑ **Check enclosed**

❑ **Visa / MasterCard / Discover / Am. Express #** _____

   Expiration   *CVV*
Signature: _____ *date:* _____ / _____ *code:* _____
          (required for credit card orders)

Colorado residents: Please add 3% sales tax.
Shipping: Include $3.95 for the first book and 75¢ for each additional book ordered.

❑ *Please send me a copy of your complete catalog of books and plays.*

Order Form

Meriwether Publishing Ltd.
PO Box 7710
Colorado Springs, CO 80933-7710
Phone: 800-937-5297 Fax: 719-594-9916
Website: www.meriwether.com

Please send me the following books:

_____ **102 Monologues for Middle School Actors** $17.95
#BK-B327
by Rebecca Young
Including comedy and dramatic monologues

_____ **101 Monologues for Middle School Actors** $16.95
#BK-B303
by Rebecca Young
Including duologues and triologues

_____ **Famous Fantasy Character Monologs** $16.95
#BK-B286
by Rebecca Young
Starring the Not-So-Wicked Witch and more

_____ **100 Great Monologs**   **#BK-B276** $15.95
by Rebecca Young
A collection of monologs, duologs and triologs for actors

_____ **102 Great Monologs**   **#BK-B315** $16.95
by Rebecca Young
A versatile collection of monologues and duologues for student actors

_____ **Ten-Minute Plays for** $17.95
Middle School Performers   **#BK-B305**
by Rebecca Young
Plays for a variety of cast sizes

_____ **More Ten-Minute Plays for** $17.95
Middle School Performers   **#BK-B319**
by Rebecca Young and Ashley Gritton
Plays for a variety of cast sizes

These and other fine Meriwether Publishing books are available at
your local bookstore or direct from the publisher. Prices subject to
change without notice. Check our website or call for current prices.

Name: _____ email: _____

Organization name: _____

Address: _____

City: _____ State: _____

Zip: _____ Phone: _____

❑ **Check enclosed**

❑ **Visa / MasterCard / Discover / Am. Express #** _____

Signature: _____   *Expiration date:* _____ / _____   *CVV code:* _____
     (required for credit card orders)

Colorado residents: Please add 3% sales tax.
Shipping: Include $3.95 for the first book and 75¢ for each additional book ordered.

❑ *Please send me a copy of your complete catalog of books and plays.*